PET

Practice Tests

Plus 3 with Key

Russell Whitehead
with Michael Black

TEACHING NOT JUST TESTING

PEARSON
Longman

Pearson Education Limited
Edinburgh Gate
Harlow
Essex CM20 2JE
England
and Associated Companies throughout the world.

http://www.pearsonlongman.com/examsplace

First published 2011

ISBN: 978 1 4082 6794 3

Set in Helvetica

Printed in Slovakia by Neografia

Acknowledgements

The publisher would like to thank the following for their kind
permission to reproduce their photographs:

(Key: b-bottom; c-centre; l-left; r-right; t-top)

Alamy Images: 19th era 118, Andrey Kekyalyaynen 114bc, Brad
Rickerby 42t, Bubbles Photolibrary 186t, 187t, Gallo Images
188t, Ian Paterson 64, Image Scotland 185t, Imageshop 42tc,
INSADCO Photography 120, LOOK Die Bildagentur der Fotografen
GmbH 17, Losevsky Pavel 186b, MBI 96b, neneo 132bc, Science
Photo Library 96c, travelib UK 117, Trinity Mirror / Mirrorpix
156, UpperCut Images 185b, vario images GmbH & Co.KG
184t, Vehbi Koca 188b, william casey 150tc; **Corbis:** arabianEye
132c, Edward Bock 114b, François Pugnet / Kipa 183b, Kate
Mitchell 132b, Sandra Eckhardt 42b, Tom Chance / Westend61
42bc; **Education Photos:** Linda Westmore 182t; **Fotolia.com:**
erikdegraaf 46, Gabriela 150b, Graca Victoria 82, Jeffrey Banke
11c, Kurhan 48, Leah-Anne Thompson 150t, Martinan 11tc,
Monkey Business 20, 96tc, Nicholas Piccillo 42c, Pambudi 84,
Paylessimages 96bc, Photo_Ma 11bc, poco_bw 114t, Rob 96t,
Serg Zastavkin 114c, Tree of life 114tc, webpictureblog.com
153, Westa Zikas 11t; **Getty Images:** Blend Images 183t, Brenda
Byrne 182b, Dejan Patic 132tc, Luca Zampedri 184b, OJO Images
187b, Soul 11b, Tetra images 132t; **Pearson Education Ltd:**
BananaStock 100, Corbis 154, Digital Vision 138, Gareth Boden
60t, 150c, Jules Selmes 78bc, 99, 150bc, Kevin Peterson 136,
Lord and Leverett 78c, MindStudio 60b, 78t, 78tc, Nigel Riches
/ Image Source Ltd 60tc, 60bc, Studio 8 60c, 78b; **Photolibrary.
com:** John Warburton-Lee 102; **Reuters:** jean-Paul Pelissier
181b; **Shutterstock.com:** 0399778584 135, pnicoledolin 66;
Thinkstock: James Woodson 181t

All other images © Pearson Education

Illustrated by Quadrum Solutions

Every effort has been made to trace the copyright holders and we
apologise in advance for any unintentional omissions. We would
be pleased to insert the appropriate acknowledgement in any
subsequent edition of this publication.

Contents

Exam Overview

The Preliminary English Test (PET) is at B1 level of the *Common European Framework of Reference for Languages*. It tests all four main skills.

PAPER 1 Reading and Writing

This paper takes 1 hour and 30 minutes.

Reading Parts 1–5

Part 1

You look at five short texts, such as signs, notes, messages, phone texts, emails, postcards, etc.

For each text, there is a multiple-choice question with three possible answers. You choose the correct answer for each question, according to the information in the text.

Part 2

You look at five descriptions of people and at eight descriptions of possible courses, films, etc. for these people.

For each person, you choose the most suitable course to study or film to see, etc.

Part 3

You read a longer text containing factual information. There is also a list of ten statements about the information in the text. Some of the statements are correct, some are incorrect.

You decide which of the statements are correct and which are incorrect.

Part 4

You read a longer text containing opinions, attitudes, experiences, etc. There are five multiple-choice questions about the text. These questions are about opinions, facts, the purpose of the text, etc.

You choose the correct answer to each question, according to the information in the text.

Part 5

You read a medium-sized text, which may contain factual information or may be a story or description.

There are ten gaps in the text, each one representing a single missing word. You look at four possible words for each gap.

You choose the correct word to fill each gap and complete the text.

Writing Parts 1–3

Part 1

You look at five sentences. Each sentence is followed by another incomplete sentence.

You write a word or words in the gap in each sentence to complete it so that it means the same as the first sentence.

Part 2

You are given a description of a situation, or a short message. This shows you what you need to do.

You write a short message, such as an email or a postcard, according to the instructions you are given.

Part 3

You are given a choice of what to do. You look at the instructions to write an informal letter containing certain information and at the instructions to write a story with a certain title or first line.

You choose which you want to write and write your letter or story.

PAPER 2 Listening

This paper takes about 30 minutes. You hear everything twice.

Part 1

You hear seven short recordings. Each one contains one person talking or two people talking together. For each recording, you look at the three pictures and the multiple-choice question with three possible answers.

You listen and choose the correct answer to each question.

Part 2

You hear a longer recording, of a talk or an interview. There are six multiple-choice questions about the factual information in the recording.

You listen and choose the correct answer to each question.

Part 3

You hear a longer recording, of one person talking. There are some incomplete sentences or notes about the information in the recording. Each gap represents one or two missing words.

You listen and write in the missing word or words in each gap.

Part 4

You hear a longer recording, of two people having an informal conversation. There are six sentences about the recording. Some of the sentences are correct, some are incorrect.

You listen and decide which sentences are correct and which are incorrect.

PAPER 3 Speaking

This paper takes 10–12 minutes. You take the test with another candidate.

Part 1

The examiner asks you and your partner questions in turn. The questions are conversation questions, such as personal information, your present situation – work, studies, etc. – past experiences and future plans.

You answer the questions, trying to give full answers.

Part 2

The examiner gives you and your partner a picture. The picture shows several things. The examiner explains a situation to you and your partner, and asks you to discuss and decide something together.

You and your partner look at the picture and discuss the situation together, making a decision as the examiner asks.

Part 3

The examiner gives your partner and you a photograph each. The topics of the two photographs are similar.

You listen to your partner talking about his or her photograph, and you talk about your photograph for about one minute.

Part 4

The examiner asks you and your partner to talk about your ideas, experiences or opinions in relation to the topic of the photographs you described in Part 3.

You listen to the examiner's questions and to what your partner says, and you talk about your ideas, experiences and opinions.

Paper 1: Reading and Writing Overview

How long is the paper?

You are given 1 hour and 30 minutes to complete this paper.

How many parts are there?

There are eight parts in total: five reading parts and three writing parts.

How long is each part?

You decide how long to spend on each part.

However, you should consider carefully how many marks there are for each part (see below).

What kinds of texts will I read?

The paper contains a range of types of text.

There are short information-based texts in Parts 1 and 2.

There are longer texts from brochures, magazines, books, etc. in Parts 3 and 4.

There is a medium-sized text from a website, encyclopaedia, etc. in Part 5.

What kind of questions are there?

The paper contains a range of question types.

There are multiple-choice questions in Parts 1, 4 and 5.

There are matching questions in Part 2.

There are correct/incorrect sentences in Part 3.

What will I have to write?

For the five reading parts, you mark your answer.

For Writing Part 1, you write a word or short phrase.

For Writing Part 2, you write a message of 35–45 words.

For Writing Part 3, you write either a letter or a story, about 100 words long.

Where do I have to write my answers?

You write all your answers on a separate answer sheet, by shading lozenges (Reading) or writing answers (Writing).

How is the paper marked?

Each correct answer to a question in the five reading parts gets one mark.

This gives you a possible total of 35 marks.

Your total mark in reading represents 25 percent of your overall exam score.

In the writing section, each correct answer to a question in Writing Part 1 gets one mark.

Writing Part 2 is marked out of 5 marks.

Writing Part 3 is marked out of 15 marks.

This gives you a total possible mark of 25.

Your total mark in writing represents 25 percent of your overall exam score.

Remember that the reading and the writing are worth the same number of marks as each other in your total exam score.

Reading Part 1: Guidance

1 Read the instructions on page 8.

1 How many questions do you have to answer?

2 What do you have to decide?

3 Where do you put your answers?

2 Look at the example.

1 What kind of text is this?
   A a notice   B an email   C a note

2 Where might you see it?

3 The correct answer is **A**. Let's decide why.
   'Charlie will get paid back by Vera for the dry cleaning later today.'
   In the text, underline the words which mean the same as:
   'get paid back'
   'later today.'

4 Why is **B** wrong? Who will take what to the dry cleaner's?

5 Why is **C** wrong? What does Vera have at the dry cleaner's? What does Charlie have at the dry cleaner's?

3 Look at Question 1.

1 What kind of text is this?
   A a sign   B a note   C a label

2 Where might you see it?

3 What might you do *before* you see it?

4 Underline the words in **A**, **B** or **C** which have the same meaning as 'while your books are checked'.

4 Look at Question 2.

1 What kind of text is this?
   A an email
   B a telephone message
   C a postcard

2 When might you receive this kind of text?

3 Underline the words in the text which you think have a positive effect.

4 Underline the words in the text which you think have a negative effect.

5 Does the word 'disadvantage' in the question relate to positive or negative things?

5 Look at Question 3.

1 What kind of text is this?
   A a note   B a phone text   C an email

2 How do you think Sandra, Betty and Paula are connected to each other?

3 Which of the sentences in the text relates to what Sandra needs to do?
   A 'Paula's emailed twice about the guest list for the party.'
   B 'Could you send it to her as soon as you can?'

4 What does 'it' refer to? 'Could you send *it* to her as soon as you can?'

6 Look at Question 4.

1 What kind of text is this?
   A a sign   B a postcard   C a note

2 Where might you see it?

3 Look at **A**. What do you usually get in a canteen? Does the text say that you can get an ID card in the canteen?

4 Look at **B**. It is correct. Why?

5 **C** is wrong. What does the text say about staff?

7 Look at Question 5.

1 What kind of text is this?
   A an email   B a phone text   C a label

2 When is the training usually?

3 Who booked training for 2 p.m. this week?

4 Who are we going to train with?

5 What time are we going to train?

Reading

Part 1

Questions 1–5

Look at the text in each question. What does it say?
Mark the correct letter **A**, **B** or **C** on your answer sheet.

Example:

0

> Charlie,
> Please can you pick up my coat from the dry cleaner's when you collect your suit? I'll give you the money this afternoon, if that's OK.
> Thanks a lot!
> Vera

What will Charlie do?

A Get paid back by Vera for the dry cleaning later today.

B Take his clothes to the dry cleaner's.

C Fetch Vera's suit from the dry cleaner's.

Answer:

1

> **RIVER SCHOOL LIBRARY**
> **Wait in this area while your books are checked.**
> **Thank you**

A You must tell us if you leave books here for checking.

B Check that you have all your books before leaving the library.

C Do not leave here until we have checked your books.

2

> Countryside here's OK.
> Mountains higher than we expected. Very limited wildlife, though the other people in the group are fun and we have easy transport.
> Deshini

In Deshini's opinion, what is the countryside's disadvantage?

A The transport.

B The animals.

C The mountains.

3

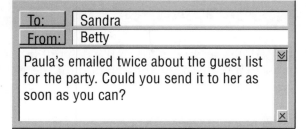

To: Sandra
From: Betty

Paula's emailed twice about the guest list for the party. Could you send it to her as soon as you can?

What does Sandra need to do?

A Let Paula know who's going to the party.

B Send a party invitation to Paula.

C Ask Paula who should be invited to the party.

4

SOUTHWOOD COLLEGE CANTEEN
Staff and students cannot use the canteen without ID cards.

A Students can get their ID cards in the canteen.

B Staff must bring their ID cards if they want to use the canteen.

C Students need to show staff their ID cards.

5

The football coach rang. Nobody from our team has booked to come at 2, only other teams. This week, to be together, we'll have to train at 4 instead.

A We need to change the training time because it's full at 2 p.m. this week.

B We may have to train with a different team this week.

C We must go training at a later time this week.

• • *Exam tip!* • • • • • • • • • • • • • • • • •

Read the text first and think about what kind of text it is. Read all three options before choosing your answer.

Reading Part 2: Guidance

1 Read the instructions on page 11.

1 How many questions do you need to answer?

2 What do all the people want?

3 What are the advertisements for?

4 How many advertisements are there?

5 What do you need to decide?

6 Where do you put your answers?

2 Look at Question 6.

1 What does Omar want to find out about?

2 Who does Omar want to meet?

3 What does Omar want to see?

4 Underline the three parts of the description of Omar that contain the information for these questions 1–3.

3 Look at Question 7.

1 What is Cecile's favourite thing to do?

2 What does she want to make better?

3 Why does she want to meet other people?

4 Underline the three parts of the description of Cecile that contain the information for these questions 1–3.

4 Look at Question 8.

1 Where does Duncan like going?

2 How does he travel?

3 What does he want to learn about?

4 Underline the three parts of the description of Duncan that contain the information for these questions 1–3.

5 Look at Question 9.

1 What does Heidi like doing?

2 Can she always do this?

3 What does she want to know about?

4 Underline the three parts of the description of Heidi that contain the information for these questions 1–3.

6 Look at Question 10.

1 What does Piotr study?

2 What do you think Piotr likes more, IT and Business or modern art?

3 Can he always go to galleries and museums?

4 Underline the three parts of the description of Piotr that contain the information for these questions 1–3.

7 Look again at Question 6.

1 Think about these words that relate to Omar's interest: architecture, building, house, home, structure … Underline words like these in the texts A–H. In which texts have you underlined words?

2 In which text have you underlined more words than other texts?

3 Does this text contain information about the three things (see 2.4 above) that Omar wants?

4 What answer should you put on your answer sheet for Question 6?

8 Look at Questions 7–10.

1 Look at the important information you underlined in the questions.

2 For each question 7–10, read through the advertisements A–H and underline words which have the same meaning as the information you have underlined in the question.

3 For each question, decide which advertisement contains the correct information which is relevant to the question.

4 Put your answers on the answer sheet.

9 Check again!

1 Why is this not correct?
   8 C

2 Why is this not correct?
   9 E

3 Why is this not correct?
   10 B

Part 2

Questions 6–10

The people below are all looking for a magazine to buy.
On page 12, there are eight advertisements for magazines.
Decide which magazine would be the most suitable for the following people.
For questions **6–10**, mark the correct letter (**A–H**) on your answer sheet.

6

Omar is interested in architecture, and wants to know more about it. He would like to meet people with the same interest, and to visit special buildings locally.

7

Cecile is very keen on sport and keeping fit, and particularly enjoys long-distance running. She would like to improve her technique, and perhaps find other people to run with.

8

Duncan enjoys spending his free time in the countryside, exploring different areas on foot and by bike. He wants to know more about what he sees when he is exploring.

9

Heidi likes going to watch her favourite football team, although she usually has to work at weekends, organising jazz concerts. She's keen to learn about the history of football.

10

Piotr is studying IT and business at university, but he's very interested in modern art, although he's usually too busy to visit galleries and museums.

> • • *Exam tip!* • • • • • • • • • • • • • • • • • •
>
> It's not enough to see that a text has something in common with one of the people – the text must contain all the things that the person needs or wants.

This Month's Pick of the Magazines

A   World of Sport
This is *the* magazine for sports fans!
All team sports are covered, with
reports on games, in case you miss
any, interviews with players and much
more. There are lots of photos and
special articles on subjects such as
the early beginnings of football and
baseball clubs in distant places.

B   History is Beautiful
Art and music lovers will really
enjoy this magazine. It's full of
interesting articles about the
history of concert music, classical
architecture around the world,
the development of the great
museums and galleries.

C   Footloose
Are you someone who loves being
outside, looking after your body?
Footloose is the magazine for the
outdoor runner who takes their hobby
seriously. Professional advice is given,
with tips for achieving the best style on
long runs. There are also lists of local
clubs you can contact or join.

D   Green World
The busier our city lives become,
the more we want to escape to the
fields and hills. *Green World* is the
magazine to take with you. There's
lots of information about birds,
animals, trees and plants, together
with maps of great bike rides and
walks to follow.

E   Sport Business
Interested in sport? Want a career in
sport? Want to study sport? This is the
magazine for you! Maybe you want to
learn about setting up a health club or
a bike shop, or about how football
clubs operate in the business world.
It's all in here.

F   Plan for Success
This magazine is all about setting
up businesses that will succeed in
today's difficult economic climate.
With articles about motivation from
famous sportspeople and tips for
running companies without waste,
you can learn all you need to
get ahead.

G   How We Live
Houses, offices, museums, bridges …
somebody designed them, somebody
built them – but most people walk
straight past them. Learn about the
structures we live and work in.
How We Live also contains a list of
local associations, so you can share
your enthusiasm with like-minded
people nearby.

H   Pictures in Your Living Room
This is the magazine for today's
art lover. Every month there are
large high-quality reproductions
of famous pictures from the 20th
and 21st centuries. Turn your
home into an exhibition hall of
these masterworks, building up
a great collection.

Reading Part 3: Guidance

1 Read the instructions on page 14.

1 How many sentences are there?

2 What are the sentences about?

3 What do you have to read?

4 What do you have to decide?

5 Are the sentences in the same order as the information in the text?

2 Look at sentences 11–20.

1 Read the sentences through to get a general idea of what they are about. How many sentences are about the *Mary Rose*, and how many about the *Golden Hinde*?

2 Match the sentences to the following topics.

a) when Drake came back to England

b) why the French were in England

c) finding out about what sailors did

d) why the *Mary Rose* disappeared

e) when a museum started

f) who was in charge of a battle

g) if a ship is original

h) what the King hoped to do

i) how many ships sailed around the world

j) what the Queen hoped would happen

3 Look at sentences 11–20 below. Match each one according to the topic to the parts of the text (a–j).

11 French ships came to England in 1545 because of the English occupation of a part of France.

12 Henry VIII decided to control the battle at Portsmouth himself.

13 Nowadays, everybody knows the reason the *Mary Rose* sank.

14 Henry VIII wanted to rescue the *Mary Rose* after it sank.

15 The Mary Rose Museum opened in 1982.

16 The *Golden Hinde* was one of three ships Francis Drake took all the way around the world.

17 Drake returned to England with a lot of money.

18 Elizabeth wanted people to visit the *Golden Hinde*.

19 The ship you can see today is the original *Golden Hinde*.

20 On the *Golden Hinde*, you can learn about how sailors found their way across the sea.

a) This ship was famous as the flagship of Sir Francis Drake during his three-year voyage around the world, with the *Golden Hinde* being the only ship to return home safely, having left in 1577.

b) As the *Mary Rose* turned, it sank. There are several different ideas about why this happened, and one day we may know for sure.

c) In 1543, Henry VIII went to war with France (not for the first time), and the next year he took control of the town of Boulogne. In response, in 1545, a large number of French ships set sail for England.

d) You can become an officer on board and find out how to navigate the *Golden Hinde* in the way the original sailors did.

e) Henry VIII, although getting old and ill, came down to take charge of the battle himself.

f) She decided that the ship should be kept so that the general public could come and look at it.

g) … 1982, when she was lifted by the Mary Rose Trust. Careful work to repair and protect the ship began. After some years, this work was completed. Now visitors can view the special collection of thousands of personal, domestic and military objects in the Mary Rose Museum.

h) The ship you can visit nowadays is a fully working model of the sixteenth-century ship.

i) When Drake came back to England, he became both rich and famous.

j) Henry tried to have the *Mary Rose* brought up from the seabed.

4 Look at your answers for 3 above. Do the sentences have exactly the same meaning (A), or a different meaning (B), as the parts of the text?

Part 3

Questions 11–20

Look at the sentences below about two old ships in the UK.
Read the text on the opposite page to decide if each sentence is correct or incorrect.
If it is correct, mark **A** on your answer sheet.
If it is not correct, mark **B** on your answer sheet.

---

11 French ships came to England in 1545 because of the English occupation of a part of France.

12 Henry VIII decided to control the battle at Portsmouth himself.

13 Nowadays, everybody knows the reason the *Mary Rose* sank.

14 Henry VIII wanted to rescue the *Mary Rose* after it sank.

15 The Mary Rose Museum opened in 1982.

16 The *Golden Hinde* was one of three ships Francis Drake took all the way around the world.

17 Drake returned to England with a lot of money.

18 Elizabeth wanted people to visit the *Golden Hinde*.

19 The ship you can see today is the original *Golden Hinde*.

20 On the *Golden Hinde*, you can learn about how sailors found their way across the sea.

> • • **Exam tip!** • • • • • • • • • • • • • • • •
> The sentences will follow the same order as the
> information in the text, but different words and
> expressions may be used in the sentences
> and text.

Ships of History

If you're interested in history or ships or both, there are two ships you must try to see in the UK – the *Mary Rose* and the *Golden Hinde*.

In 1543, **Henry VIII** went to war with France (not for the first time), and the next year he took control of the town of Boulogne. In response, in 1545, a large number of French ships set sail for England. The French had over 200 ships in their fleet, and the English about 80, waiting near the town of Portsmouth on the South Coast. The leading ship was the ***Mary Rose***, the biggest and best ship in England at that time. Henry VIII, although getting old and ill, came down to take charge of the battle himself.

The French ships couldn't get into Portsmouth, because it was defended by towers and a castle, but they started firing at the English fleet. The English ships moved towards the French, but, as the *Mary Rose* turned, it sank. There are several different ideas about why this happened, and one day we may know for sure.

Although Henry tried to have the *Mary Rose* brought up from the seabed, she remained underwater until 1982, when she was lifted by the Mary Rose Trust. Careful work to repair and protect the ship began. After some years, this work was completed. Now visitors can view the special collection of thousands of personal, domestic and military objects in the Mary Rose Museum. With so much to see, you're sure to have an interesting time!

You could also come to London and see the ***Golden Hinde***. This ship was famous as the flagship of Sir Francis Drake during his three-year voyage around the world, with the *Golden Hinde* being the only ship to return home safely, having left in 1577.

Drake captured many Spanish ships during the voyage, and took their gold and money. When Drake came back to England, he became both rich and famous. Queen Elizabeth I took a share of the prizes captured, and visited the *Golden Hinde* with great ceremony. She decided that the ship should be kept so that the general public could come and look at it, making it England's first museum ship.

The ship you can visit nowadays is a fully working model of the sixteenth-century ship, and has also sailed around the world. If history and sailing interest you, then attend a special workshop on the *Golden Hinde*. For the afternoon, you can become an officer on board and find out how to navigate the *Golden Hinde* in the way the original sailors did before modern electronic equipment was invented. Yes, you can travel through the past!

Reading Part 4: Guidance

1 Read the instructions on page 17.

1 What do you have to read?

2 What do you have to do?

3 How many possible answers are there for each question?

4 Where do you mark your answers?

2 Read the text quickly and answer:

1 What activity is the writer mainly talking about?

2 What did the writer think about camping when he was a child?

3 Where did the writer go camping when he was a child?

4 Does the writer think campsites are the best places to stay in?

5 Who does the writer go camping with these days?

3 Read Questions 21–25. Then, in 1–5 below, <u>underline</u> the best word or phrase to complete each sentence.

1 Question 21 asks about *where / when / why* the writer wrote the text.

(This is always a general question.)

2 Question 22 asks about the writer's *job / life / friends*.

(This is always a question about detail or opinion.)

3 Question 23 asks about *opinion / experience / ability*.

(This is always a question about detail or opinion.)

4 Question 24 asks about a *plan / hope / comparison*.

(This is always a question about detail or opinion.)

5 Question 25 asks about what the writer *has said / will say / would say*.

(This is always a general question.)

4 Look at sentences a–e, taken from the text. Put them in the order in which they appear in the text.

a) I think every family should have that.

b) But they have great showers and shops, and are reasonable value for money.

c) My father worked for the oil industry and my family moved from city to city.

d) We could see they loved it: the freedom, cooking on a fire, looking at the stars at night.

e) The message for families is clear.

5 Look again at Questions 21–25.

1 Question 21

Look at these extracts from the text:

Camping … a life-long enjoyment; I loved camping then and I still, therefore, do today; I think every family should have that [= camping holidays]; I like to think that they [= children] understood the value …

a) Which two of the function words do these extracts seem most related to?

b) Look at **A**. Does the writer really tell us what to do when getting ready to go camping?

c) Look at **B**. Does the writer say camping is a good thing to do and want other people to do it?

d) Look at **C**. Does the text mainly contain detail about the writer's childhood holidays?

e) Look at **D**. Does the writer think children should go camping without their parents?

2 Question 22

The answer is **D**. Can you <u>underline</u> the part of the text that includes this information?

3 Question 23

The answer is **A**. Can you <u>underline</u> the part of the text that includes this information?

4 Question 24

The answer is **A**. What are the 'simple things' in the text?

5 Question 25

a) Why are A, B, D wrong?

b) The answer is C: can you <u>underline</u> the part of the text that contains this information?

Part 4

Questions 21–25

Read the text and questions below.
For each question, mark the correct letter **A**, **B**, **C** or **D** on your answer sheet.

To Camp or Not to Camp

When I asked a group of my friends this question, everybody had a strong opinion. Camping was either terrible or wonderful – there was nothing in between. It depends on childhood: if you had fun camping when you were a kid, then that was the beginning of a life-long enjoyment. But the opposite could also be true! The message for families is clear.

Personally, I loved camping then and I still, therefore, do today. My father worked for the oil industry and my family moved from city to city. I was quite lonely, I realise now. I never felt that the holidays we spent in other cities were real holidays; real holidays were the ones when we got out into the countryside and slept in tents. I think every family should have that. And even though I still live and work in a big city, this remains my opinion.

The camping I remember was out there, up mountains, in forests, by rivers – not stuck in campsites. If you're camping with friends or family, that's who you want to be with, not all the other people you meet in campsites. They're too safe. But they have great showers and shops, and are reasonable value for money. In fact, a night at a site once in a while lets you all get your clothes clean and stock up with food. But, wherever you go, don't pack lots of things: keep it basic and you'll have a better time.

We took my children camping last summer. We could see they loved it: the freedom, cooking on a fire, looking at the stars at night. I like to think that they understood the value of fresh air and water, sunshine, running and swimming, and that it meant more to them than expensive beach holidays.

21 What is the writer's main purpose in writing the text?

   A   To explain how to prepare for a camping trip.

   B   To encourage families to go camping together.

   C   To describe his childhood camping experiences.

   D   To persuade parents to let their children go camping.

22 What does the writer say in the second paragraph?

   A   He spent a lot of time with his parents when he was young.

   B   He had a happy childhood.

   C   He has always taken his holidays in the countryside.

   D   He has always lived in cities.

23 What does the writer say about campsites?

A   It is useful to stay at campsites occasionally.

B   It is too expensive to stay at campsites.

C   They don't usually have enough facilities.

D   They are a good place to make friends.

24 What does he hope his children learnt on their last camping holiday?

A   The importance of simple things.

B   How to save money.

C   The names of stars.

D   How to cook food.

25 What is the writer most likely to say?

A
If you go camping, take a map that shows where campsites are.

B
People don't always realise that camping is enjoyed most by children.

C
The less you take with you when camping, the more you'll enjoy it.

D
Remember that camping can be quite dangerous, so plan your trip carefully.

•• **Exam tip!** •••••••••••••••••••
You need to look at the whole text when you answer Questions 21 and 25. You need to read particular parts of the text to answer Questions 22, 23 and 24.

Reading Part 5: Guidance

1 Read the instructions on page 20.

1 What do you have to read?

2 What do you have to choose?

3 How many choices do you have for each question?

4 Where do you mark your answers?

2 Read through the text.

1 Is it factual or is it a story?

2 Is it difficult to understand what the text is about?

3 Are there any questions about the overall meaning of the text?

4 Is it a long text or a short text?

3 Look at the questions. Do you feel sure of some of the answers already?

1 Look at Question 26. You need to read around the gap here. You need to notice that there are two things, home and work. Which preposition is used to link two things like this?

2 Look at Question 27. Which of the possible answers means a physical thing as well as a situation in geography?

3 Look at Question 28. Which of the answers means 'similar to'?

4 Look at Question 29. Which of the answers refers to the idea of possibility, of the writer not knowing for sure?

5 Look at Question 30. Which of the answers is closest in meaning to 'live'?

6 Look at Question 31. You need to complete the phrase here: 'more and ....' . Which of the answers will help to complete the phrase so that it means 'an increasing number'?

7 Look at Question 32. You need to notice the word 'as' here. Which of the possible answers would be correct in this sentence: 'I was .... my newspaper as an umbrella because it had started raining suddenly'?

8 Look at Question 33. 'that this is a better way to work': this clause is the same as 'something'. Which of the possible answers can you put before 'something'?

9 Look at Question 34. Which word means the same as 'acceptable', as, for example, in the sentence: 'This film isn't .... for young children'?

10 Look at Question 35. Which word means 'planned and made for a particular purpose'?

4 Look at the questions again. This time, choose a different answer for the gap in each new sentence 1–10 below. Note: more than one answer is possible in two of these sentences.

1 Look at Question 26. I didn't see her because she was standing .... the door.

2 Look at Question 27. We keep the dictionaries in this .... of the library.

3 Look at Question 28. He talks .... quickly that I can't understand him.

4 Look at Question 29. You .... take your coat because it's really cold out there.

5 Look at Question 30. I want to .... a small farm when I'm older.

6 Look at Question 31. It's .... more than I can afford.

7 Look at Question 32. I'm .... a lot of money, but I find my job quite boring.

8 Look at Question 33. Please .... them about what we've decided to do.

9 Look at Question 34. Planning is very important for a business to be ....

10 Look at Question 35. Alexander Bell .... the telephone.

Part 5

Questions 26–35

Read the text below and choose the correct word for each space.
For each question, mark the correct letter **A**, **B**, **C** or **D** on your answer sheet.

Example:

| **0** | **A** For | **B** By | **C** From | **D** To |

Answer:

| 0 | **A** ■ | **B** ☐ | **C** ☐ | **D** ☐ |

Working from Home

(0) .... most people with jobs, some of the day is spent travelling **(26)** .... the home and the **(27)** .... of work. This can feel **(28)** .... a waste of time, but perhaps you can't afford to live near your office. Or you **(29)** .... want to have a big garden or **(30)** .... in the same neighbourhood as your family.

However, more and **(31)** .... people are changing their lives. They are working from home, **(32)** .... a room as their office, connected to their company by the internet. They **(33)** .... that this is a better way to work. They can work harder and they feel less tired.

If you want to do this, make sure you have a **(34)** .... room to work in, with a well **(35)** .... desk and chair. Of course, don't watch TV — and don't work for *too* long!

26	**A** among	**B** behind	**C** across	**D** between
27	**A** part	**B** position	**C** point	**D** place
28	**A** like	**B** so	**C** that	**D** as
29	**A** must	**B** may	**C** should	**D** can
30	**A** have	**B** become	**C** set	**D** be
31	**A** many	**B** much	**C** more	**D** most
32	**A** making	**B** doing	**C** using	**D** putting
33	**A** say	**B** inform	**C** tell	**D** speak
34	**A** correct	**B** suitable	**C** right	**D** successful
35	**A** designed	**B** invented	**C** discovered	**D** formed

Writing Part 1: Guidance

1 Read the instructions on page 22.

1 How many sentences are there?

2 What are the sentences about?

3 What do you need to do?

4 How many words can you use?

5 Where do you write your answers?

6 What do you write there?

7 Where can you do your rough work?

2 Compare the two sentences in the example.

1 Read the first sentence. What happens after people see Machu Picchu?

2 Now read the second sentence. What happens after people see Machu Picchu?

3 Does the second sentence give you the same information as the first sentence?

3 Answer Question 1.

1 Read the first sentence. What information does it give you about Machu Picchu?

2 Now read the second sentence. How does it begin? How does it end?

3 How can you complete it? Write your answer.

4 Check your answer.

• Does your completed second sentence give the same information as the first sentence?

• Is the grammar correct?

• How many words have you used?

5 Answer the other questions in the same way.

It is probably better to write your answers in rough on the exam paper first. When you have checked them carefully, you should copy them onto the answer sheet.

6 Match each pair of sentences in the Exam Task with these examples of patterns. Some sentences contain two patterns.

a) Adverbs with opposite meanings.

b) Pronouns with opposite meanings.

c) Active verb ☐ passive verb.

d) If + not ☐ unless.

e) Not as + adjective = less than.

f) Irregular verb forms.

g) Verbs with opposite meanings.

h) There is/are ☐ has/have/contains.

7 Checking your work: read these sentences from other Writing Part 1 questions. There is a mistake in each second sentence. Can you correct the mistakes?

1 When I was younger, I often went camping.
   When I was younger, I use to go camping.........

2 I drove all the way there by myself.
   I drove all the way there by my own...........

3 I was able to repair my bike this morning.
   I succeeded in repair my bike this morning......

4 One of my classmates lent me this book.
   A classmate of me lent me this book.............

5 I arrived here an hour ago.
   I'm here for an hour............................

Writing

Part 1

Questions 1–5

Here are some sentences about a place called Machu Picchu.
For each question, complete the second sentence so that it means the same as the first.
Use no more than three words.
Write only the missing words on your answer sheet.
You may use this page for any rough work.

Example:

0   Nobody ever forgets seeing Machu Picchu.

   Everybody always .... Machu Picchu.

Answer:

0	remembers seeing

---

1   Machu Picchu is probably the most important historical site in South America.

   Other historical sites in South America are probably not .... as Machu Picchu.

2   Plants and trees hid the ancient city from people for hundreds of years.

   The ancient city .... from people by plants and trees for hundreds of years.

3   The site contains the remains of many different buildings.

   There .... the remains of many different buildings at the site.

4   The tourist train to the site doesn't travel very quickly.

   The tourist train travels .... to the site.

5   If Machu Picchu isn't protected, tourists will damage it.

   Tourists will damage Machu Picchu .... is protected.

• • *Exam tip!* • • • • • • • • • • • • • • •
Use what you know about grammar to help you:
try to see what pattern is being tested in each
sentence. As you study and practise, build up a
list of patterns.
• •

Writing Part 2: Guidance

1 Read the instructions on page 24.

1 What are you going to write?

2 Who are you going to write to?

3 How many things do you need to write about?

4 How many words do you need to write?

5 Where do you write your answer?

2 Planning your answer.

1 Why are you writing the postcard?

2 What will you say first in your postcard?

3 Why do you like it? Which verb tense will you use in your answer to this point?

4 What did you do on your birthday? Which verb tense will you use in your answer to this point?

3 Look at the postcard below. Choose the correct words to fill each gap.

> **(1)**............ Julie,
>
> Thank you so much for the lovely present you sent me **(2)**............ my birthday!
>
> You know The Curios are my favourite band – I've **(3)**............ played it twenty **(4)**............ .
>
> My birthday **(5)**............ fun. I went **(6)**............ a pizza restaurant with about six friends.

Love

1	A For	B Dear
2	A at	B for
3	A already	B still
4	A ways	B times
5	A was	B had
6	A to	B in

4 Understanding instructions. In Writing Part 2, you need to write different kinds of messages. Look at these instructions from other Reading Part 2 tasks, and match them to the sentences a–g below.

0 invite somebody to do something

1 promise to do something

2 explain the reason why you can't do something

3 accept an invitation to do something

4 persuade somebody to do something

5 suggest going somewhere with somebody

6 refuse an invitation to do something

a) I can't help you with your computer because I don't know anything about computers.

b) Would you like to come to a party at my parents' house next Saturday?

c) I'm sorry, but I won't be able to come to the football match.

d) I'd love to come shopping with you and your sister.

e) Why don't we all go to the beach at the weekend?

f) I'll make sure I bring your bike back by six o'clock.

g) Please change your mind and say you'll come to the cinema with us.

5 Sentence structure. Match parts of sentences 1–5 with the missing parts a–e.

1 I had such a great time staying with

2 I think we should buy her some

3 Is it easy to find the way to

4 I recommend you bring some

5 What is your favourite subject at

a) your house or do I need a map?

b) school at the moment?

c) DVDs for her birthday present.

d) you last week.

e) warm clothes with you.

Part 2

Question 6

Your English friend, Julie, sent you a birthday present.

Write a postcard to send to Julie. In your card, you should

- thank her for the present

- explain why you like it

- describe what you did on your birthday.

Write **35–45 words** on your answer sheet.

• • Exam tip! • • • • • • • • • • • • • • • • • • •
You MUST write about all THREE of the points in your answer.
• •

Writing Part 3: Guidance

1 Read the instructions on page 26.

1 How many questions do you answer?

2 How many words do you write?

3 Where do you write your answer?

4 Where do you put the question number?

2 Read Question 7 and Question 8.

1 Write down three ideas for your letter.

2 Write down five useful words or phrases that you can use in your letter.

3 Quickly think of a story that you could write.
   - What can happen in the second sentence?
   - What will happen after that?
   - How will it end?

4 Write down five useful words or phrases that you can use in your story.

3 Choose which question you will answer.

1 Look at your notes.

2 Do you have enough ideas for the letter? Do you know the vocabulary you need?

3 Can you write your story in 100 words? Do you know the vocabulary you need?

4 Which of these questions seems easier for you?

4 Look at this example of an answer to Question 7. For each gap, choose the missing phrase from the box.

always seems to	a little strange
that you like	so much	with more news
one if you can	more than hear

Dear Dave
Thanks for your letter.
It's interesting **(1)**............ going to the cinema **(2)**............ , because I really like it too!
The films I like may sound **(3)**............ to you. I love films made by Jacques Tati, a French director working in the 1950s and 1960s. They are very funny, but the jokes are ones you see **(4)**............ : there isn't a lot of talking. The main character in these films is Jacques Tati himself, and he **(5)**............ make terrible mistakes!

Try to see **(6)**............ .
Write soon **(7)**............ .

5 Look at this example of an answer to Question 8. For each gap, choose the missing phrase from the box.

fell over	and carefully	been here for
had forgotten		banging noise
had left		across the room

I was glad when the phone started to ring. I thought Gina **(1)**............ all about me. I ran **(2)**............ to answer, but my brother **(3)**............ so many things everywhere – clothes, books, a football. I **(4)**............ . When I got to the phone, it stopped ringing. What should I do? Then I heard a loud **(5)**............ . It was the front door. I was scared, but I went to see. The banging continued. Slowly **(6)**............ , I opened the door a little way. There was Gina. 'Your doorbell doesn't work,' she said. 'I've **(7)**............ ages! Why didn't you answer your phone?'

Part 3

Write an answer to **one** of the questions (**7** or **8**) in this part.
Write your answer in about **100 words** on your answer sheet.
Mark the question number in the box at the top of your answer sheet.

Question 7

- This is part of a letter you receive from an English penfriend.

> I really like going to the cinema. What kinds of film do you like? Tell me about them. Why do you like them?

- Now write a letter to your penfriend about films.

- Write your **letter** in about 100 words on your answer sheet.

Question 8

- Your English teacher has asked you to write a story.

- Your story must begin with this sentence:

I was glad when my phone started to ring.

- Write your **story** in about 100 words on your answer sheet.

· · *Exam tip!* · · · · · · · · · · · · · · · ·
Try to include a good range of vocabulary and grammar in your answer: making a list when you plan can help you to make sure you show the examiner what you know.
· ·

Paper 2: Listening Overview

How long is the paper?

You are given about 30 minutes to complete this paper. When the recordings finish, you are given 6 minutes to copy your answers from the question paper onto your answer sheet.

How many parts are there?

There are four parts.

How long is each part?

Each part takes a few minutes.

Each part is repeated and you will hear all the instructions.

There are pauses to give you time to read and understand the instructions and the questions, and also to check your answers.

The times are controlled by the recording, so you do not have to decide how long to spend on each part.

What will I listen to?

You will listen to recordings of native speakers.

There will be speakers with a range of accents, and of different ages.

The situations may be neutral or informal.

You may hear just one person speaking in some recordings, and conversations between two people in other recordings.

Some recordings may be on the phone, others may be on the radio. Many will be in houses, shops, etc.

What kinds of questions are there?

In Part 1, there are separate multiple-choice questions with three possible answers.

In Part 2, there is a series of multiple-choice questions, each with three possible answers.

In Part 3, there are sentences or notes with gaps.

In Part 4, there is a series of correct or incorrect sentences.

How many times will I hear the recordings?

Twice.

What will I have to write?

In Parts 1, 2 and 4, you choose a letter as your answer and put a tick (✓) in a box.

In Part 3, you write a word or words that you hear in the recording to fill each gap.

Where do I have to write my answers?

You write on the separate answer sheet, either by shading lozenges (Parts 1, 2 and 4) or writing answers (Part 3).

In all parts, you can put your answers on the question paper while you are listening.

When the recordings finish, you can copy your answers onto the separate answer sheet.

How is the paper marked?

Each correct answer to a question gets one mark.

This gives a possible total of 25 marks.

Your total mark in listening represents 25 percent of your overall exam score.

Part 1: Guidance

1 🎧 **Listen to the introduction to the test.**

1 How many parts does the listening test have?
2 How many times will you be able to listen to each part?
3 What should you do before each part of the test?
4 What should you do after each part of the test?
5 Where do you write your answers?
6 What will you do at the end of the test?
7 How long will you have to do this?

2 🎧 **Read and listen to the instructions for Part 1 on page 29.**

1 How many questions are there?
2 How many pictures are there for each question?
3 What do you need to do?

3 Look at the example question and the three pictures.

1 What is the same in the three pictures?
2 What is different in the three pictures?

4 🎧 **Listen to the recording for the example.**

1 Why is **A** the correct answer?
2 Why is **B** wrong?
3 Why is **C** wrong?

5 Look at Questions and pictures 1–7.

1 What are the times shown on the three watches? Can you think of more than one way of saying each time?
2 What can you see in each picture?
3 Practise telling somebody how to go from the house to the school by each route, A, B and C.
4 What are the different objects in the pictures?
5 What are these things called?
6 What can you see in each picture?
7 What are these three machines? What are they used for?

6 🎧 **Listen to each question. Look at the following extracts from the audioscript and the box of missing words. Choose the correct word for each gap.**

couple	for	only	fallen	ahead
plates	till	farm	like	have
	behind	never		

1 Question 1. OK, OK, but the film isn't .... half past, is it?
2 Question 2. I think the elephant is the one to go .... because it's another wild animal, while the horse is more of a .... animal maybe.
3 Question 3. I turn right when I come out of my house, and then go on till I .... to go left, and then school's just .... along the road.
4 Question 4. Sure – a .... of cartons?
5 Question 5. But I realised when I took my towel out that I .... put my toothbrush in, ... the toothpaste – which is pretty useless now!
6 Question 6. A tree has .... across the street, and there are lorries that can't pass, so now all the cars are stuck .... them and can't move at all.
7 Question 7. Well, I turned it on, so that I could wash the .... , but now water's coming out of it .... out of the shower.

Part 1

Questions 1–7

There are seven questions in this part.
For each question, there are three pictures and a short recording.
Choose the correct picture and put a tick (✓) in the box below it.

Example: Which are Sara's cousins?

 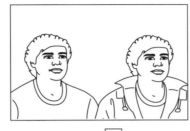 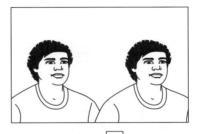

A ✓   B ☐   C ☐

---

1 What time does the film start?

A ☐   B ☐   C ☐

2 Which picture does the boy want?

 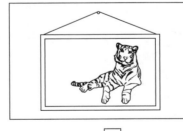 

A ☐   B ☐   C ☐

· · **Exam tip!** · · · · · · · · · · ·
· Remember that you hear everything twice
· in the test, so you have time to check
· your understanding.
· ·

3 How does Valentina get from her house to school?

A ☐   B ☐   C ☐

4 What does Sally need?

A ☐   B ☐   C ☐

5 What did the man forget to pack?

A ☐   B ☐   C ☐

6 What problem is there in the town?

A ☐   B ☐   C ☐

7 What needs to be repaired?

A ☐   B ☐   C ☐

Listening Part 2: Guidance

1 🎧 **Read and listen to the instructions on page 32.**

1 How many questions are there?
2 Who will you hear?
3 What will he talk about?
4 What do you need to do?
5 How many times will you hear the recording?

2 🎧 **Listen to the recording. Which question below, a or b, does the interviewer ask Ronald?**

1 a Did you walk a long way every day?
   b How far did you go each day?
2 a Did you have to prepare?
   b Did you need to prepare?
3 a Was there any particular reason for starting there?
   b Did you have a particular reason that you started there?
4 a And where did you sleep?
   b Where did you go to sleep?
5 a What did you enjoy most about the walk?
   b What was the best thing about the walk?
6 a What did you plan?
   b And what's that?

3 🎧 **Listen to the recording and look at Questions 8–13.**

1 For Question 8:
   A Which day did Ronald walk 11 miles?
   C How many days did he walk 18 miles?
2 For Question 9:
   A Did he need to walk up hills or mountains?
   B When did he go on a long walk?
3 For Question 10:
   B Where was the sun when he started walking each day?
   C When did the weather improve?
4 For Question 11:
   A When did he stay in a guesthouse?
   C How often did he stay in a campsite?
5 For Question 12:
   A Did he like the scenery?
   B What did he think about the animals?

6 For Question 13:
   B What does he say about his holiday?
   C Did he intend to plan a talk?

4 🎧 **Read each question and the box of missing words. Listen to the following extracts from the recording. Choose the correct word for each gap.**

before	thought	along	Mostly	myself
night	helps	then	every	put	else

1 .... it was around 13 miles.
2 I took fitness classes nearly .... day, and did a long walk a week .... I started the coast-to-coast walk, to make sure I was ready for it.
3 The wind generally comes from behind you, so it .... you – sometimes it was so strong it blew me .... !
4 I took a tent with me, and spent a .... in a campsite, though I generally .... it up close to the path, wherever I was walking.
5 I suppose the best thing was having some time to .... with no one .... around.
6 I intended to plan the talk while I was walking, but .... I had the idea of writing a book about walking in Scotland, and I .... about *that* most of the time, instead.

Part 2

Questions 8–13

You will hear a radio interview with Ronald Ferguson, who has just walked across Scotland from coast to coast. For each question, put a tick (✓) in the correct box.

---

8   How far did Ronald usually walk each day?

- **A**   About 11 miles. ☐
- **B**   About 13 miles. ☐
- **C**   About 18 miles. ☐

9   How did Ronald prepare for the walk?

- **A**   He climbed several mountains. ☐
- **B**   He went walking every weekend. ☐
- **C**   He went to fitness classes. ☐

10   Ronald started in Oban because

- **A**   the wind made walking easier. ☐
- **B**   the sun was usually behind him. ☐
- **C**   the weather was better than in the east. ☐

11   Where did Ronald usually sleep?

- **A**   In guesthouses. ☐
- **B**   Beside the path. ☐
- **C**   In a campsite. ☐

12   What did Ronald enjoy most about the walk?

- **A**   The scenery. ☐
- **B**   Watching animals. ☐
- **C**   Being alone. ☐

13   During the walk Ronald planned

- **A**   a book. ☐
- **B**   a holiday. ☐
- **C**   a talk. ☐

> **Exam tip!**
> Reading through the questions before you listen will help to give you an overall understanding.

Listening Part 3: Guidance

1 🎧 **Read and listen to the instructions on page 34.**

1 Who will you listen to?

2 What will this person be talking about?

3 What do you need to do?

4 How many times will you hear the recording?

2 Read the Exam Task. Think about the kind of information you will need to write in each gap.

1 Question 14: will you write a subject or a year?

2 Question 15: will you write an adjective or a noun?

3 Question 16: will you write a number or a noun?

4 Question 17: will you write a name or a noun?

5 Question 18: what is likely to go here?

6 Question 19: what is likely to go here?

3 Look at the Exam Task below. The answers are wrong, although all the words used are in the recording.

> *School Trip to Cardiff*
> *Mainly for students of (14)* Wales .
>
> *First day: visit to Welsh Assembly*
> *Tour of the building.*
> *Talk by a government minister about the Assembly and improvements to (15)* parliament .
>
> *Second day:*
> *Morning: tour of Cardiff Castle and chance to learn about (16)* castle *in the Middle Ages.*
> *Afternoon: talk by member of City Council about the protection of (17)* public .
>
> *Practical information:*
> *Dates: 22–25 June*
> *Travel: by coach to Swindon and then by (18)* return .
> *Accommodation: in a (19)* stadium .

Here are the correct answers, jumbled up. Can you decide which gap each word should go in?

hostel	medicine	wildlife	transport
	train	politics	

14 ....

15 ....

16 ....

17 ....

18 ....

19 ....

🎧 **Now listen and check your answers.**

4 Look at these extracts from the recording. Which word is correct for each gap?

1 This trip will be of particular interest to those of you *studying / learning* politics, though if there are any spare places, other people can go too.

2 She'll also discuss plans to *increase / improve* transport, which is one of her own areas of responsibility.

3 Then you'll join in an activity that'll teach you about medicine in the *period / time* when much of the castle was built, the Middle Ages.

4 He'll talk to us about various *ideas / projects* for protecting wildlife, and show us some of the improvements over the last few years.

5 We'll travel by coach to Swindon, and take the train from there to Cardiff – the whole journey will take *over / around* two hours.

6 And we'll *spend / book* three nights in a hostel.

🎧 **Now listen and check your answers.**

Part 3

Questions 14–19

You will hear a teacher talking to a group of schoolchildren about a school trip.
For each question, fill in the missing information in the numbered space.

School Trip to Cardiff

Mainly for students of (14) ....

First day: *visit to Welsh Assembly*
....

Tour of the building.

Talk by a government minister about the Assembly and improvements to

(15) ....

Second day:

Morning: tour of Cardiff Castle and chance to learn about

(16) .... in the Middle Ages.

Afternoon: talk by member of City Council about the protection of

(17) ....

Practical information:

Dates: 22–25 June.

Travel: by coach to Swindon and then by

                    (18) ....

Accommodation: in a (19) ....

· · *Exam tip!* · · · · · · · · · · · · · · ·
Usually you write one word, but you may have
to write two or even three, but never more than
that. Answers may be numbers too.
· ·

Listening Part 4: Guidance

1 🎧 **Read and listen to the instructions on page 36.**

1 How many sentences are there?

2 How many people will you hear?

3 What is the boy called?

4 What is the girl called?

5 What are they going to talk about?

6 What do you need to do?

7 How many times will you hear the conversation?

2 Read the six sentences.

1 Which sentences are about Max?

2 Which sentences are about Max and Jenni?

3 Which sentences are about the future?

4 Which sentence is about the past?

3 Read questions 1–9 below. 🎧 **Listen to the recording and answer the questions.**

1 When do they need to book a restaurant?

2 Jenni says some classmates want to go to a .... restaurant.

3 What's the name of the Chinese restaurant?

4 Who's going to the Chinese restaurant?

5 What's the Mexican restaurant called?

6 What has Jenni heard about the Mexican restaurant?

7 There will be at least .... people going to the restaurant.

8 Can everybody afford somewhere expensive?

9 Max wants to make a .... of restaurants.

4 Look at the Exam Task below. Match the words and phrases underlined in sentences 20–25 with the words and phrases a–f taken from the recording. Some of these will have the opposite meaning!

20 Max wants to have the food that he <u>usually eats</u>.

21 The Chinese restaurant will be <u>closed</u>.

22 They <u>have both been</u> to the Mexican restaurant.

23 Max wants to go to a restaurant with <u>live music</u>.

24 They agree to set a <u>fixed price</u> for the meal.

25 The <u>whole class</u> will choose the restaurant.

a) I remember going to some place with a singer and guitarist, and it was great.

b) It won't be open for our dinner.

c) Make the decision ourselves.

d) I eat it at least twice a week.

e) I never went there.

f) Why don't we fix the amount and ask a restaurant to provide a meal for that price?

5 Look at the extracts below from the recording. They are jumbled up. Can you put the words in them into the right order?

1 must really we the book soon restaurant

2 mean I you what see

3 you about what

4 be that yeah could problem a

5 good a idea that's

🎧 **Now listen and check your answers.**

Part 4

Questions 20–25

Look at the six sentences for this part.
You will hear a girl, Jenni, and a boy, Max, planning dinner in a restaurant for their class.
Decide if each sentence is correct or incorrect.
If it is correct, put a tick (✓) in the box under **A** for **YES**.
If it is not correct, put a tick (✓) in the box under **B** for **NO**.

		A YES	B NO
20	Max wants to have the food that he usually eats.	☐	☐
21	The Chinese restaurant will be closed.	☐	☐
22	They have both been to the Mexican restaurant.	☐	☐
23	Max wants to go to a restaurant with live music.	☐	☐
24	They agree to set a fixed price for the meal.	☐	☐
25	The whole class will choose the restaurant.	☐	☐

> • • *Exam tip!* • • • • • • • • • • • • • • •
> Because many of the questions are about whether
> the two speakers agree or disagree, you need to
> listen very carefully to what they say.

Paper 3: Speaking Overview

How long is the paper?

Your speaking test will be 10–12 minutes long.

You will take the test with another candidate.

How many parts are there?

There are four parts.

How long is each part?

Parts 1 and 2 take 2–3 minutes each.

Parts 3 and 4 take 3 minutes each.

What kinds of questions are there?

The questions are different in each part of the speaking test.

In Part 1, the examiner will ask you straightforward questions about your life and experiences.

In Part 2, the examiner will ask you and your partner to discuss something together, using a picture to help you.

In Part 3, the examiner will ask you to speak about a photograph for about a minute.

In Part 4, the examiner will ask you and your partner to discuss some ideas and opinions together.

Who will be in the room?

You and your partner will sit together.

There will be one examiner who speaks to you, gives you the pictures, etc.

There will be another examiner who will not speak to you. He or she will be marking you and your partner throughout the test.

How is the paper marked?

You are marked on your speaking throughout the speaking test. The mark you get will be based on several things.

- The grammar and vocabulary you use.
- The way you organise what you say.
- Your pronunciation.
- The way you communicate with your partner and the examiner.
- How well you do the tasks overall.

The total possible mark is 25.

Your total speaking mark represents 25 percent of your overall exam score.

Watch the full test on your DVD.

TEST 1

Part 1: Guidance

Conversation. Match these examiner questions 1–10 and possible student answers (a–j) below.

1 What's your name?
2 What's your surname?
3 How do you spell it?
4 Do you work or are you a student?
5 What do you study?
6 What did you do last weekend?
7 Do you think English will be useful to you in the future?
8 Tell us about your English teacher.
9 How do you travel to school every day?
10 What do you do in your spare time?

a) Business studies, with English and French.
b) Usually by bus, but sometimes my brother drives me.
c) Alex.
d) I'm a student, but I have a part-time job.
e) She's very patient, and she tells us a lot of jokes.
f) Cagol.
g) Nothing special: I saw my parents, and spent some time in the park with my friends.
h) C-A-G-O-L.
i) Actually, I don't have very much spare time, but I like cycling and I go to the cinema when I can.
j) Well, I hope so! Yes, I want to work for an international company, and I think my English will be essential.

Part 2: Guidance

Look at the picture on page 173 [The picture for Test 1 Speaking Part 2], and at the instruction the examiner gives you on page 39. Speaking together. Match the expressions (1–10) used when speaking together about the task with the functions (a–e) below.

1 How about having a party like this?
2 Do you mean with loud music?
3 Maybe it would be too noisy, so you couldn't talk together.
4 I guess you're right.
5 Do you think it's a good idea to have a picnic together in the park?
6 That sounds good.
7 Or we could go to the cinema?
8 I'm not sure about that idea.

9 Do you mean it's not a good idea?
10 All right, let's do that.

a) making a suggestion
b) disagreeing with a suggestion
c) checking understanding
d) asking for your partner's opinion
e) agreeing with a suggestion

Part 3: Guidance

Read this student's description of a picture. Choose the correct word to fill each gap.

This is an interesting picture. I can (1) look / see two people. (2) I'm not sure I / I don't agree what they're doing exactly, but I think they (3) may / ought be making bread, or (4) several / some other kind of food. They look quite old, (5) because / so perhaps it's a traditional kind of cooking. They (6) sound / seem to be enjoying what they're doing. They're both laughing. You can (7) know / tell from the window that it's very sunny outside. Perhaps (8) it's / there's going to be a big party (9) later / after, and they're preparing (10) for / to it.

Part 4: Guidance

Read this text about a student talking about what she does in her spare time. Choose words and phrases from the box to fill the gaps.

to do that   each other   I guess   what I want really depends on   If   and maybe   for example because that's the time   Sometimes

When I get home from school I like having dinner with my family (1) .... we can sit together. We talk about our day, what happened. Sometimes we ask (2) .... for advice about some problem, (3) .... It's nice. After dinner, we often do different things. (4) .... I go over to see my friends by bike, and we just relax together. (5) .... it's cold or raining, then I stay at home, (6) .... play computer games or watch TV. It (7) .... my mood. Anyway, if I have a lot of homework, then I need (8) .... But in the summer holidays, for example, then I can do (9) .... I prefer that – not surprising, (10) .... !

Part 1

Take turns to be the examiner. Ask your partner questions to find out some information about each other.
Ask each other at least four of these questions:
- What's your name?
- What's your surname?
- How do you spell it?

- Where do you come from?
- Are you a student or do you work?
- What do you do/study?
- Do you enjoy studying English?
- Do you think you will use English in the future?
- Did you do anything last weekend?
- What do you enjoy doing in your free time?

Part 2

Your examiner gives you and your partner a picture. You do a task together.

Look at page 173. An English language club is planning to celebrate its tenth anniversary. Talk together about the different things they can do to celebrate the tenth anniversary, and then decide which one would be best.

Ask and answer questions like these:
- Which activities will be most popular with the members?
- Do you think this one is a good idea?
- How many people will come to the celebrations?
- Do you think it's better to be indoors or outdoors?
- Which one shall we say is the best idea?

Part 3

You take turns to talk to each other about a photograph.

Candidate A: Look at Photograph 1A on page 181.
Candidate B: Look at Photograph 1B on page 185.

Think about your photograph for a few seconds. Describe it to your partner for about one minute. Tell your partner about these things:
- where the people are
- what they are doing
- what they might be saying
- what they might be feeling
- what you can see as well as people.

Part 4

The examiner asks you to talk to your partner. Talk to each other about computers.

Use these ideas:
- Say what you use computers for.
- Talk about whether you enjoy using computers.
- Say where you use computers.
- Talk about who you use computers with.

Reading

Part 1

Questions 1–5

Look at the text in each question.
What does it say?
Mark the correct letter **A**, **B** or **C** on your answer sheet.

Example:

0

> Charlie,
> Please can you pick up my coat from the dry cleaner's when you collect your suit? I'll give you the money this afternoon if that's OK.
> Thanks a lot!
> Vera

What will Charlie do?

A Get paid back by Vera for the dry cleaning later today.

B Take his clothes to the dry cleaner's.

C Fetch Vera's suit from the dry cleaner's.

Answer:

1

| To: | Carlos |
| From: | Lisa |

Good holiday? When you're back at college, don't forget to sign up for the language course. Tell me if you need some more information about it.

Why has Lisa contacted Carlos?

A To tell him about her holiday.

B To remind him to do something.

C To give him some details.

2

£30 TO RESERVE ANY PHOTOGRAPH IN THE EXHIBITION

A You must pay £30 if you want to display photographs.

B We will keep a photograph for you, if you pay £30.

C Some of the photos in the exhibition are reserved.

3

Elsa,
So nice to see you last night! I meant to ask you more about your new job. Brilliant! I'm sure you're pleased!
Let's have lunch soon.
Shakeh

What is Shakeh doing in this card?

A   Offering Elsa her congratulations.

B   Providing some new information.

C   Thanking Elsa for her lunch.

4

COLLEGE HOLIDAYS
After next Thursday, the Study Centre will be closed during evenings and weekends.

The Study Centre will

A   open again for students on Friday.

B   open for fewer hours until Thursday.

C   change its opening hours from Thursday.

5

We're staying at the Regent Hotel. It's not the one we tried to book first, but it doesn't matter: this one's actually nearer the beach — where I'm spending all my time!
Keiko

What does Keiko feel about the Regent Hotel?

A   She wishes it was closer to the beach.

B   She prefers another hotel to it.

C   She thinks it has an advantage.

. . **Exam tip!** . . . .
Be very careful when you are transferring your answers from the question paper to your answer sheet.
. . . .

Part 2

The people below all want to watch a TV programme.
On the opposite page, there are descriptions of eight TV programmes.
Decide which programme would be most suitable for the following people.
For questions **6–10**, mark the correct letter (**A–H**) on your answer sheet.

6

Rita and Patsy are interested in dance. They like both modern and traditional ballet, and enjoy learning about the dancers' experiences and ideas. They often go out in the evening.

7

Charlie and Petra are very keen on nature, particularly wildlife and the Antarctic. They enjoy experts discussing environmental issues, but they don't like phone-in programmes.

8

Roger and Martin both go cycling every weekend, entering short- and long-distance races. They want to be as fit as possible and also learn about the history of cycle racing.

9

Penny and Paul enjoy live arts, especially theatre and classical music concerts. They live in the countryside and cannot go to the city very often.

10

Dani and Fred are interested in exploration, especially people who go on trips for the first time or in unusual ways. They would like to plan a trip themselves one day.

> **• • Exam tip! • • • • • • • • • • • • • • • • •**
> • Remember you cannot use any letter more than
> • once, so there will be unused texts when you
> • have finished.

TV Programmes

A Stage Sensational

Three young actors play in this new evening series about a drama club. Keen to escape from the traditional approach of the school, they develop their own modern style – but can they manage to show it in public performances?

B One Man and His Bike

The longest journey: whether this is your first viewing or you are returning to keep up-to-date, you'll be entertained by Harry Lomas' self-recorded commentary. Harry describes his strange experiences as he rides around the world on his old red bike, following routes nobody's tried before. Tonight he meets a bear.

C Animal Access

If you're concerned about green issues, if you care about wild animals, here's the programme for you. Join our panel discussion by phoning in with your questions or suggestions for keeping our planet safe for animals, and you could even win the top prize: a trip to Antarctica.

D Moving Story

Follow the joys and heartaches of a junior dance school's attempts to reach the national final championships in different styles. Every afternoon, you can see an update of their progress, and you can phone in your vote on individual performances.

E The Road to Success

An enjoyable biography of one of the fastest cyclists of all time. Mixing old sections of film with current interviews – and even the chance to phone in with your own questions about technique and so on – this programme will inspire you to ride faster yourself.

F The Last Paradise

The white frozen landscape of the South Pole is said to be the last place man hasn't damaged beyond repair. Watch the fascinating filming of native animals and birds. You'll feel you're there yourself with some of the never-before-used camera techniques.

G Perfect Performances

Whether your tastes are traditional or more modern, you'll love this celebration of plays and operas, each one performed to the highest standards and broadcast to your living room. Additional material about history and background is available interactively.

H Routes and Riding

For children and parents alike, this programme is designed to get children riding bikes, exploring the countryside, getting fitter and healthier and learning more about the natural world around them. Special routes are shown for first-time riders.

Part 3

Questions 11–20

Look at the sentences below about cycling holidays.
Read the text on the opposite page to decide if each sentence is correct or incorrect.
If it is correct, mark **A** on your answer sheet.
If it is not correct, mark **B** on your answer sheet.

---

11   You will get advice about correct ways of cycling.

12   Food during the day is provided free of charge.

13   You do not have to carry your own bags or suitcases on your bike.

14   The distance you cover changes according to how hilly or flat the roads are each day.

15   You can go on a tour of a lake in a boat.

16   Different standards of hotel may be used each night.

17   It costs more if you want to stay in a single room.

18   You can choose what kind of meal you want to eat in the evening.

19   All groups are smaller than 15 in number.

20   Children under 14 can come on these holidays with their parents.

Blue Sky Cycling Holidays

Wondering where to go for your holidays this year? Tired of beach holidays? Do you feel that just lying on some sand is not the most interesting way to spend your precious holiday time? Want a holiday with a bit more zing? If your answer is 'yes' to these questions, then the solution is obvious: join us on a Blue Sky Cycling Holiday!

Get fit while you relax on holiday. Every cycling group is joined by two of our expert guides and tour leaders. As well as being great fun, they are qualified fitness trainers, so they will make sure you cycle in the right way. What you eat is, of course, up to you! We will be passing through villages with very special local foods for your lunch, so you can buy what you prefer.

And don't worry about trying to carry all your luggage on your bike, as this will be taken from hotel to hotel in our cars, to be ready for you every night. The distance we cover each day will depend on the kind of countryside we're travelling through, so you'll never get too tired. Our routes are carefully planned to include lots of places of interest, with frequent breaks to enjoy a coffee or a tour of an old castle or a rest by the side of a lake.

Accommodation is arranged for you in good-quality 3-star hotels. Experience has taught us that this is the standard most people prefer on our holidays. Our prices are per person, based on sharing a twin room, but single accommodation is available for a small extra payment at the time of booking. There is a choice of breakfasts, from tea and fruit to complete cooked breakfasts, and, similarly, in the evenings, you can help yourself from a buffet or go for the set menu.

In order to keep the groups friendly and also safe along the roads, we set a limit on the number of people on a holiday. This varies to some extent depending on the landscape and road types being used on any particular holiday, but we don't run holidays with fewer than six guests or more than fifteen. In addition, we set a limit on children of no more than five in any group, and they must be accompanied by at least one parent. We also hope you will understand that these holidays aren't suitable for children under the age of fourteen.

Call or email for more information or to make a booking today!

Part 4

Read the text and questions below.
For each question, mark the correct letter **A**, **B**, **C** or **D** on your answer sheet.

By Design

Years ago, when I first thought of becoming a designer, people just didn't seem to be as interested in design. These days, there's always some series on TV about design. There are all sorts of qualifications you can get. Actually, we've had designers all the way through our history. They have made pyramids, scientific instruments, things to sit on, clothes to wear … Nowadays, a lot of IT designers seem to think they are kings or emperors, that their work is the most interesting work there is.

Boats can be quite a good way of understanding this point. Sea transport was one of the crucial things we learnt to do – we spread our population, we got new kinds of food and raw materials. It's amazing to think how far people explored in ancient boats. Modern boats are packed with sophisticated computer equipment to help sailors find their way, avoid storms and so on, yet we found our world without all that. Pay attention to those old boats: they float, they move in the right direction, *and* they have pretty patterns, nice colours. We want things to look good and work well.

Food raises the same issues. Many of us have moved from hands to tools for cooking and eating with, finding new ways to make the process easier. In the West, people have knives and forks; in the East, they have chopsticks – unlike each other in appearance, but they do a similar job. Throughout history, great value has always been placed on the appearance of these tools. This is why we need and depend on design, linking our past and present, country with country, and why we will continue to do so.

21 What is the writer's main purpose in writing the text?

   A To encourage people to try to become designers.

   B To list the different stages in the history of design.

   C To explain why most people do not like design.

   D To show the general importance of design in the world.

22 What do we learn about the writer from the text?

   A   He thinks some designers are too proud.

   B   He always wanted to be a designer.

   C   He thinks there should be more designers.

   D   He wants to make TV programmes about design.

23 What point is made about boats?

   A   Ancient boats were very sophisticated.

   B   Boat design mixes practical and visual issues.

   C   Modern boats are not beautiful to look at.

   D   Few boats are used for exploring.

24 The writer says that tools for eating

   A   have changed very little over time.

   B   are often not very easy to use.

   C   look different in different cultures.

   D   have become more important socially in recent years.

25 What would a reader of the text say?

A
Transport and food have always been regarded as the two most important types of design.

B
It's disappointing to realise that a large number of designers are not professionally qualified.

C
It's exciting to think how much effect computers are going to have on design in the future.

D
There are several different things to think about when you look at how something is designed.

> **. . Exam tip! . . . .**
> Remember that sometimes you are looking for
> information about facts, and sometimes about opinions,
> so make sure you understand each question.

Part 5

Questions 26–35

Read the text below and choose the correct word for each space.
For each question, mark the correct letter **A**, **B**, **C** or **D** on your answer sheet.

Example:

0   **A** seems   **B** reviews   **C** looks   **D** supposes

Answer:

0	A	B	C	D
	■	☐	☐	☐

In Tune

It **(0)** .... music is almost as old as human life itself. If we knock two things **(26)** .... at regular intervals, for example, we like the **(27)** .... It has a meaning **(28)** .... us.

Music has the power to change how we feel. It can **(29)** .... us excited – and it can **(30)** .... sadness. In our minds, we connect certain pieces of music with particular people or places.

However, sometimes we almost **(31)** .... to realise the effect of music. For example, **(32)** .... you watch a TV programme or a film, there's often music playing – maybe for the **(33)** .... of the time – and it tells you, in an indirect way, that something dangerous is going to **(34)** .... , or that this is a romantic moment, and so on. But many people can hardly **(35)** .... the music at the end of the programme.

26	**A** ahead	**B** together	**C** alike	**D** next
27	**A** result	**B** end	**C** final	**D** answer
28	**A** at	**B** on	**C** for	**D** by
29	**A** make	**B** do	**C** put	**D** go
30	**A** design	**B** invent	**C** discover	**D** create
31	**A** lose	**B** fall	**C** miss	**D** fail
32	**A** when	**B** how	**C** then	**D** where
33	**A** master	**B** majority	**C** matter	**D** maximum
34	**A** set	**B** take	**C** happen	**D** become
35	**A** fasten	**B** remind	**C** forget	**D** remember

> **. . Exam tip! . . .**
> It's a good idea to read through the whole text quickly first, to get a general idea of what it's about, before starting the questions.

Writing

Part 1

Questions 1–5

Here are some sentences about moving house.
For each question, complete the second sentence so that it means the same as the first.
Use no more than three words.
Write only the missing words on your answer sheet.
You may use this page for any rough work.

Example:

0 Ian moved to his new house two weeks ago.

   Ian's lived in his new house .... **two weeks.**

Answer:	**0**	*for*

---

1 His new house is taller than the other houses in the street.

   His new house is .... **house in the street.**

2 His old friend Fred lives in the same street.

   Fred, an old friend .... **, lives in the same street.**

3 There's a beautiful view from Ian's balcony.

   Ian's balcony .... **a beautiful view.**

4 He had a rather small house before.

   He .... **to have a rather small house.**

5 He was given help moving by his family.

   His family .... **help moving.**

· · *Exam tip!* ·
It's not enough just to put in a word or words that fit
grammatically. You must read your completed second
sentence carefully to make sure it has the same *meaning*
as the first sentence.

Part 2

Question 6

You want to spend Saturday with your friend.

Write an email to your friend. In your email, you should

- ask if your friend is free

- explain what you want to do together

- suggest where to meet.

· · Exam tip! · · · · · · · · · · · · · · ·
Read your email through and imagine you are the person receiving it. Will you understand everything? Will you be happy to receive it?
· ·

Write **35–45 words** on your answer sheet.

Part 3

Write an answer to **one** of the questions (**7** or **8**) in this part.
Write your answer in about **100** words on your answer sheet.
Mark the question number in the box at the top of your answer sheet.

Question 7

- This is part of a letter you receive from an English friend, Peter.

> My uncle has given me some money. I want to spend it on buying computer games. My parents say I should save the money. What do you think?

- Now write a letter to Peter, answering his question.

- Write your **letter** in about 100 words on your answer sheet.

Question 8

- Your English teacher has asked you to write a story.

- This is the title for your story:

An amazing conversation

· · Exam tip! · · · · · · · · · · · · · · · ·
This is an important part of the test. Make sure you leave enough time to write your answer as well as you can: you should allow 20–25 minutes.
· ·

- Write your **story** in about 100 words on your answer sheet.

Part 1

Questions 1–7

There are seven questions in this part.
For each question there are three pictures and a short recording.
Choose the correct picture and put a tick (✓) in the box below it.

Example: Which are Sara's cousins?

  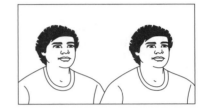

A ✓　　　　　B ☐　　　　　C ☐

---

1 Which is the family's holiday house?

A ☐　　　　　B ☐　　　　　C ☐

2 What sport is recently available at the sports centre?

A ☐　　　　　B ☐　　　　　C ☐

3 Where is the man's wallet?

 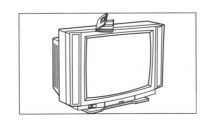 

A ☐　　　　　B ☐　　　　　C ☐

4 When did David's aunt leave?

A ☐

B ☐

C ☐

5 Which photo are they talking about?

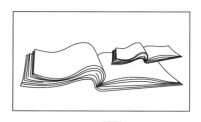

A ☐

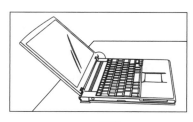

B ☐

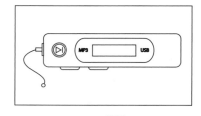

C ☐

6 What will the woman take on the train journey?

A ☐

B ☐

C ☐

7 How much will the boy pay for a ticket for the football match?

BEES **50-50** Matchday Draw
£10
☆ 1st Prize of 50% of net takings
☆ 2nd Prize £25
BRENTFORD

A ☐

BEES **50-50** Matchday Draw
£12
☆ 1st Prize of 50% of net takings
☆ 2nd Prize £25
BRENTFORD

B ☐

BEES **50-50** Matchday Draw
£14
☆ 1st Prize of 50% of net takings
☆ 2nd Prize £25
BRENTFORD

C ☐

*• • **Exam tip!** • • • • • • • • • • • • • • • • • • •*

Before the recordings start, look carefully at the
pictures for each question and try to understand what
they show.

Part 2

Questions 8–13

You will hear a woman called Tina making a radio report about her recent trip to Africa.
For each question, put a tick (✓) in the correct box.

---

8   What does Tina say about the weather during her trip?

    A   It rained almost every day.   ☐

    B   It was too hot in the day.   ☐

    C   It was very cold at night.   ☐

9   The first journey Tina made was

    A   in a small plane.   ☐

    B   on foot.   ☐

    C   by a special car.   ☐

10   Tina was surprised when they saw

    A   a crocodile.   ☐

    B   a lizard.   ☐

    C   a hippopotamus.   ☐

11   Tina liked how close they got to

    A   an elephant.   ☐

    B   some zebras.   ☐

    C   different birds.   ☐

12   Tina recommends visiting Zambia on safari most to

    A   young people.   ☐

    B   couples with children.   ☐

    C   retired people.   ☐

13   Tina says she will never forget

    A   the sunsets.   ☐

    B   the people she saw.   ☐

    C   the sense of space.   ☐

> **· · Exam tip! ·**
> Remember that the order of the questions is the same as
> the order of the information in the recording. If you miss
> one the first time, you can check it the second time.

Part 3

You will hear a man giving a talk about a sports event to raise money for charity.
For each question, fill in the missing information in the numbered space.

Mini Olympic Games

Location: Greenford Primary School

Closing date for entries: (14) ....

Aims: to raise money for medical research.

          to raise money for new (15) ....

          to encourage children in sport.

First event starts: (16) ....

Parents to ensure children have enough (17) ....
on the day.

Most popular event expected to be (18) ....

More children needed for the (19) .... event.

> **Exam tip!**
> The words and numbers that you need to write in the
> gaps are all ones that you hear in the recording: don't
> change what you hear.

Part 4

Questions 20–25

Look at the six sentences for this part.
You will hear a mother, Marina, and her son, Sam, talking about hobbies.
Decide if each sentence is correct or incorrect.
If it is correct, put a tick (✓) in the box under **A** for **YES**.
If it is not correct, put a tick (✓) in the box under **B** for **NO**.

		A YES	B NO
20	Marina thinks Sam has fewer hobbies than his friends.	☐	☐
21	Sam thinks indoor hobbies are boring.	☐	☐
22	Sam thinks he's good at playing table tennis.	☐	☐
23	Marina enjoyed cycling when she was a child.	☐	☐
24	Marina suggests Sam joins a sports club.	☐	☐
25	Sam may spend his pocket money on a new hobby.	☐	☐

> **Exam tip!**
> Pay attention to the situation. You can read it at the beginning of this part and you
> will hear it in the recording. It is important to understand who the speakers are
> and why they are talking about something together.

Part 1

General conversation: saying who you are, spelling your name, giving personal information.

Take turns to be the examiner. Ask your partner questions to find out some information about each other.

Ask each other:
* What's your name?
* What's your surname?

* How do you spell it?
* Where do you come from?
* Are you a student or do you work?
* What do you do/study?
* Which season of the year do you like most?
* What places would you like to visit in the future?

· · **Exam tip!** ·
Make sure you are familiar with the sorts of questions you might be asked in this part.
If you don't understand what's going on, you may become nervous in the test.

Part 2

Simulated discussion: exchanging opinions, saying what is necessary.

Your examiner gives you both a picture. You do a task together.

Your school has got some money to buy more equipment to help the students. Look at page 174. Talk together about the different things that the school could buy and decide which ones would be the most useful for students.

Ask and answer questions like these:
* Do you think X will be useful for students?
* How expensive will X be to buy?
* Which things do you consider to be most helpful?
* How will the students use this, do you think?

· · **Exam tip!** ·
Talk about your ideas. Don't just give an opinion: explain your reasons for this opinion too.

Part 3

You take turns to tell each other about a photograph.

Candidate A: Look at Photograph 2A on page 181.
Candidate B: Look at Photograph 2B on page 185.

Think about your photograph for a few seconds.
Describe it to your partner for about one minute.

Tell your partner about these things:
- where the people are
- what they are trying to do
- how they feel about what they are doing
- what the man's job probably is
- what sort of pictures they are probably looking at.

• • *Exam tip!* •
Make sure you speak clearly in this part: don't sit too closely over the photograph.

Part 4

The examiner asks you to talk to your partner.

Talk to each other about taking and looking at photos.

Use these ideas:
- Say how often you take photographs.
- Say what you take photographs of.

- Say how important you think it is to take photographs.
- Say what you think about photographs of famous people in newspapers and magazines.
- Say if you would like to be a professional photographer. Why/Why not?

• • *Exam tip!* •
Remember that this part is a discussion between you and your partner. Don't try to include the examiner in your conversation.

Reading

Part 1

Questions 1–5

Look at the text in each question.
What does it say?
Mark the correct letter **A**, **B** or **C** on your answer sheet.

Example:

0

> Charlie,
> Please can you pick up my coat from the dry cleaner's when you collect your suit? I'll give you the money this afternoon if that's OK.
> Thanks a lot!
> Vera

What will Charlie do?

A Get paid back by Vera for the dry cleaning later today.

B Take his clothes to the dry cleaner's.

C Fetch Vera's suit from the dry cleaner's.

Answer:

0	A	B	C
	▬	▭	▭

1

> **SPORTS CLUB GYM**
> **Please put all practice equipment back in this room before you leave.**

A Remember to take your equipment with you when you leave.

B You shouldn't take any equipment outside this room when you go.

C We leave some equipment at the back of this room for practising.

2

> I'm here in London today with Chris, who's at a job interview at the moment. It's raining, so I'm visiting museums. We're catching the train home together tonight.
>
> **Jenny**

A Chris is staying overnight in London, but Jenny isn't.

B Jenny is writing this text while Chris attends an interview.

C Jenny and Chris are spending the day together sightseeing.

3

GREAT SPORTS BIKE

In perfect condition – less than two years old – quick sale needed – offers welcome (not less than €100).

Abdul 0775 221 321

A   Abdul's bike needs only a few repairs.

B   Abdul bought this bike two years ago.

C   Abdul would accept €100 for his bike.

4

Shop delivery vehicles unload here 08.00 a.m. – 10.00 a.m. daily. Customer parking permitted at any other time.

A   Customers may park here when vehicles are not unloading.

B   Customers may park outside the shop for up to two hours.

C   You may unload your delivery vehicle here after ten o'clock.

5

To   All students
From   College Office

Please note that student identity cards will be available for collection from 25 September.

A   Students should bring their identity cards with them on 25 September.

B   Student identity cards are only available until 25 September.

C   The first day students can pick up identity cards is 25 September.

Part 2

Questions 6–10

The people below all want to do a training course.
On the opposite page there are eight advertisements for training courses.
Decide which training course would be most suitable for the following people.
For questions **6–10**, mark the correct letter (**A–H**) on your answer sheet.

6

Heinrich studies economics at university but has decided he wants to work in the media in future. His economics lectures are in the mornings and he goes to nightclubs most evenings.

7

Lily works in a fashionable clothes shop and would like to become a manager there, but she needs to improve her ability to use computers. The shop is open every day until 6 p.m.

8

Abigail doesn't have a job at the moment, but she would like to work in a sports centre, perhaps as a coach to a team. She is keen on keeping fit and swims every day.

9

Lin wants to learn more about business so that he can run his own shop one day. He's studying languages at university and has a part-time job as an assistant in a sports shop.

10

Lena is interested in style and fashion, particularly interior design. Her current job is in a music shop, where she works every evening.

Advertisements for training courses

A On this useful course, you'll learn how to **manage others** and bring out the best in any group. The course is relevant to a wide range of work situations, particularly hospitality, sports and entertainment. It's a full-time and demanding course, with expert teachers and proven results.

B High street or street market, clothes, furniture or jewellery: whatever you sell, you can learn to sell more of it. The internet is still largely misunderstood by most business people, so make sure you're ahead of the game with this evening course in **IT systems and online selling**, and improve your chances of success.

C **Music** is a fashionable business to be in right now, and you can increase your chances by learning some important techniques. With our special course structure, you can choose when and where to study, putting you firmly on the path to success.

D Use our **computer-based course** to help you achieve your dreams. Fashion is an international language, but you need language skills to succeed in it. Our specialist course will provide you with valuable practice, so you can communicate your creative ideas.

E Sport and leisure are growing parts of the economy at present. You can ensure your place in their future with our special international **sports sector certificate course**, which includes important topics such as marketing and health and safety for sports centre management. You need to have relevant employment experience.

F Are you creative? Are you ambitious? This course will help you get ahead in the competitive world of creative business, where you need to be super-fit to win. Join our course of morning classes, and learn how to start up a business, perhaps a shop or consultancy.

G This course is perfect for people who have a basic understanding of **business** but who want to explore the possibilities of TV, newspapers, the internet and so on as their career. This is a part-time course, with classes three afternoons a week.

H Do you wish to be your own boss? Need to know how? Many ambitious and skilled people find they have some experience and perhaps a strong academic background, but feel they need specific knowledge about **marketing and finance** to ensure their success when selling to the public.

Part 3

Look at the sentences below about a photography website.
Read the text on the opposite page to decide if each sentence is correct or incorrect.
If it is correct, mark **A** on your answer sheet.
If it is not correct, mark **B** on your answer sheet.

---

11   Associate members get a discount when buying equipment.

12   If you recommend a friend to become a member they will pay less.

13   You cannot speak to an expert in person at the Advice Centre.

14   You must include details of the manufacturer if asking about camera repairs at the Advice Centre.

15   You need to be a member if you want to take part in the competition.

16   Check on the website to find out what subject to use for photos in the competition.

17   Full members may send no more than three photos each month to the gallery.

18   The number of photos shown in the gallery increases regularly.

19   You can add your ideas to others on the blog.

20   If you pay more, the things you buy from the online shop will arrive more quickly.

Home News Gallery About Us Contact

Search

Welcome to the home page of the *Photography World* website. We offer a range of useful services for photographers and photography lovers.

Camera Club

Join our club and enjoy a range of benefits. You will get invitations to our regular events, such as members' film shows, exhibitions and talks by experts. You can apply for Full membership, Associate membership or Junior membership. Full membership includes free entry to all events and 10% discount when ordering equipment online. Associate membership gives you half-price tickets to events. Junior membership (proof of age required) is a cheap way to enjoy the benefits of Full membership. Costs (per year): Full £20, Associate £12, Junior £10. Most of our members have joined as the result of recommendations from current members.

Advice Centre

Take advantage of our Advice Centre. Ask our panel of experts your questions about cameras and photography. Whether you're looking for solutions to problems or fresh ideas for interesting photos, you'll get a good response here. Simply email your question to advice@cameraclub.com or leave a recorded message on 0800 565656. We guarantee to send you a reply by email within five days. Please note that we cannot provide information about repairs to particular cameras, and that you should contact the manufacturer about these.

Competition

Our competition is held every year and is a great chance for new and experienced photographers to win one of our great prizes, which range from books to keep your photos in to one-day courses to a set of state-of-the-art camera equipment. Entries can only be accepted from members, and can be sent in as prints, on a CD or memory stick or by email. Please note photos cannot be returned, so make sure you have copies. The topic – for example, wildlife, transport, people – is announced each year here on the website when the competition opens.

Gallery

This is a great opportunity to show your photos. All full members can send in up to six photos each month, from which we will choose two or three to display in the gallery section of the website. More photos are added every month, so keep watching this exciting part of the site.

Blog

This is a great opportunity to show your photos. All full members can send in up to six photos each month, from which we will choose two or three to display in the gallery section of the website. More photos are added every month, so keep watching this exciting part of the site.

Shop

Our popular online shop is the place to buy equipment, spare parts, film, memory cards … You can be sure of high quality, fair prices and quick delivery. We even offer the choice of 12-hour Super Express service for a small extra charge.

Part 4

Read the text and questions below.
For each question, mark the correct letter **A**, **B**, **C** or **D** on your answer sheet.

My Job: John Knight, Architect

I can honestly say that architecture is the only job I ever thought of having. At school, I wasn't really thinking about what to do afterwards. I enjoyed science and art subjects, and got on well with my teachers, who often lent me extra books to study. My mum and dad suggested I train as an architect, and I just went along with their idea.

I'm glad I did. It's a great job, connecting engineering, art, people and the places we all live and work in. Clients – our word for customers – of course, are the people who make it all happen. Some I get on with, some not. I have to balance what they say they want – and they usually know that very definitely – with what is or isn't possible on a practical level. I invite them to explain the project as they see it developing, and then try to explore ways forward from there.

So there are the meetings, then the designing itself, and also the researching, the checking, dealing with builders and so on. It's a good mixture of activities. And, of course I'm developing all the time as a person, learning new ways of doing things. Ever since I started out as a young architect, I've tried not to look back, but to keep finding new solutions. I've built all sorts of buildings, with my favourite so far being a hospital – which is basically a hotel for the ill – and the job I'm really hoping to get is the new intercity station that will be built on the site of the old museum here in the centre.

21 What is John Knight trying to do in the text?

   A Persuade people to hire him as their architect.

   B Explain the difference between good and bad architecture.

   C Describe the working life of an architect.

   D Compare being an architect with doing other jobs.

22 Why did John Knight become an architect?

   A He was good at science subjects at school.

   B His art teacher suggested it.

   C He enjoyed looking at books about buildings.

   D His parents encouraged him.

23 What does John Knight say about his clients?

    A   They usually have a practical approach.

    B   They often have strong ideas about what they want.

    C   They are usually difficult to work with.

    D   They change their minds quite often.

24 What does John Knight want to design?

    A   a hospital

    B   a station

    C   a museum

    D   a hotel

25 What are John Knight's clients most likely to say about him?

A
> He started by asking us to tell him our ideas about what the building should look like when it's finished.

B
> He likes to compare different buildings he has designed with each other, to see if this gives him new ideas.

C
> He never really intended to become an architect, but he has learnt to enjoy working with a wide range of clients.

D
> He believes he produced his most interesting designs when he was young and keen to try different things.

Part 5

Read the text below and choose the correct word for each space.
For each question, mark the correct letter **A**, **B**, **C** or **D** on your answer sheet.

Example:

0	**A** famous	**B** known	**C** favourite	**D** leading

Answer:

0	**A** ■	**B** ☐	**C** ☐	**D** ☐

Sharks

Sharks are very **(0)** .... fish. The film *Jaws* was **(26)** .... several years ago, and gave millions of people a fear **(27)** .... sharks. It was about a Great White Shark, the biggest of **(28)** .... sharks, at over 3 metres and up to 3,000 kilograms.

It's not known exactly how **(29)** .... sharks live, but scientists think at least 30 years. They have a top **(30)** .... of about 40 kilometres. They are known to swim **(31)** .... one continent and another in a single year.

People **(32)** .... don't need to be so scared of sharks. Humans aren't attractive to sharks as food, because they prefer animals with more fat and less bone. When sharks attack humans, it's usually **(33)** .... they thought they were another kind of animal. **(34)** .... 1867, there have been only about 224 attacks on people – one or two a year in the world. Meanwhile, people have killed a **(35)** .... larger numbers of sharks than that.

26	**A** done	**B** discovered	**C** made	**D** invented
27	**A** to	**B** with	**C** of	**D** from
28	**A** whole	**B** every	**C** all	**D** each
29	**A** old	**B** long	**C** far	**D** late
30	**A** run	**B** distance	**C** run	**D** speed
31	**A** between	**B** against	**C** further	**D** beside
32	**A** very	**B** rather	**C** indeed	**D** really
33	**A** why	**B** because	**C** how	**D** so
34	**A** During	**B** When	**C** Since	**D** For
35	**A** much	**B** lot	**C** many	**D** great

Writing

Part 1

Questions 1–5

Here are some sentences about Mount Everest.
For each question, complete the second sentence so that it means the same as the first.
Use no more than three words.
Write only the missing words on your answer sheet.
You may use this page for any rough work.

Example:

0   Mount Everest is higher than any other mountain in the world.

    Mount Everest is .... mountain in the world.

Answer:

0	the highest

---

1   Mount Everest is such a high mountain that it is very difficult to climb.

    Mount Everest is .... high that it is very difficult to climb.

2   The top was first reached in 1953 by two climbers.

    The top was reached for the .... by two climbers in 1953.

3   There is too little oxygen at the top of Everest to breathe easily.

    There isn't .... oxygen at the top of Everest to breathe easily.

4   At only 13, Jordan Romero climbed Everest in May 2010.

    Jordan Romero .... 13 when he climbed Everest in May 2010.

5   It costs a lot of money to climb Everest.

    Climbing Everest .... expensive.

Part 2

Question 6

You weren't able to meet your friend yesterday to go to the cinema together.

Write an email to your friend. In your email, you should

- apologise for not meeting your friend

- explain why you couldn't meet your friend

- suggest how to meet next.

Write **35–45 words** on your answer sheet.

Part 3

Write an answer to **one** of the questions (**7** or **8**) in this part.
Write your answer in about **100 words** on your answer sheet.
Mark the question number in the box at the top of your answer sheet.

Question 7

- This is part of a letter you receive from an English friend, Claire.

> I want to get a holiday job. I can stay with my parents and work in an office, or work in a hotel at the seaside and stay in the hotel. What do you think I should do?

- Now write a letter to Claire, answering her question.

- Write your **letter** in about 100 words on your answer sheet.

Question 8

- Your English teacher has asked you to write a story.

- Your story must begin with this sentence:

  As the woman got off the bus, John saw that her laptop was still by her seat.

- Write your **story** in about 100 words on your answer sheet.

Part 1

Questions 1–7

There are seven questions in this part.
For each question, there are three pictures and a short recording.
Choose the correct picture and put a tick (✓) in the box below it.

Example: Which are Sara's cousins?

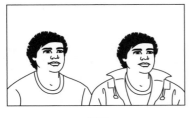

A ✓

B ☐

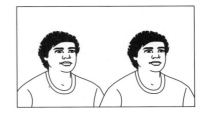

C ☐

---

1 What did Juan enjoy on holiday?

A ☐

B ☐

C ☐

2 Where will the woman go first after work?

A ☐

B ☐

C ☐

3 Which is the new flat?

A ☐

B ☐

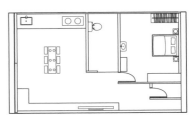

C ☐

4 When do they decide to have lunch?

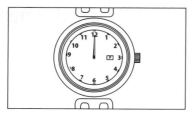

A ☐

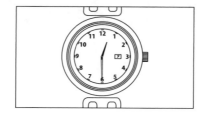

B ☐

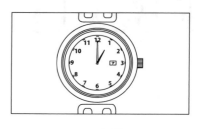

C ☐

5 Which jacket does Harry want to buy?

A ☐

B ☐

C ☐

6 Which postcard do they decide to send?

A ☐

B ☐

C ☐

7 How will they travel to the airport?

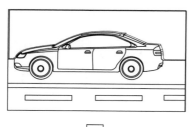

A ☐

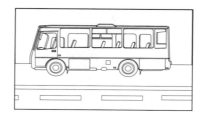

B ☐

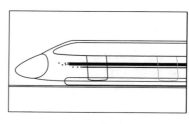

C ☐

Part 2

Questions 8–13

You will hear an interview with a man called Robbie, who works as a courier, delivering things by bicycle in London.
For each question, put a tick (✓) in the correct box.

8   Robbie became a bike courier because

    A he didn't like being a student. ☐

    B his friends encouraged him. ☐

    C he was unable to find another job. ☐

9   What happened when he went for his interview?

    A He arrived very late. ☐

    B It was difficult to find the office. ☐

    C Everybody seemed very friendly. ☐

10   What was a problem on his first day?

    A A parcel was too big to carry. ☐

    B His bike broke down. ☐

    C He went to the wrong address. ☐

11   Robbie thinks that many riders feel

    A competitive. ☐

    B independent. ☐

    C stressed. ☐

12   Robbie says many couriers are surprised that they don't

    A learn more about the geography of London. ☐

    B spend much time with the other couriers. ☐

    C get as tired as they had expected to. ☐

13   What advice does Robbie give about becoming a bicycle courier?

    A Make sure you have a very good bike. ☐

    B Do it for a limited period of time. ☐

    C Study a street map of London. ☐

Part 3

Questions 14–19

You will hear a woman talking about a festival.
For each question, fill in the missing information in the numbered space.

Honeyford Festival

Festival for town of Honeyford and surrounding countryside

Honeyford Festival first held in the year
(14) ....

Last year there were record numbers of
(15) ....

TV programme crew will film the show of traditional
(16) ....

There will be a demonstration of making
(17) ....

You can take part in a (18) .... class.

A family ticket costs (19) £ ....

Part 4

Questions 20–25

Look at the six sentences for this part.
You will hear a girl called Marta and a boy called Jim talking about the holidays they are going to have.
Decide if each sentence is correct or incorrect.
If it is correct, put a tick (✓) in the box under **A** for **YES**.
If it is not correct, put a tick (✓) in the box under **B** for **NO**.

		A YES	B NO
20	Marta's parents want to go to Scotland.	☐	☐
21	Jim would like to go skiing.	☐	☐
22	Jim's brother is hoping to invite a friend to come on holiday.	☐	☐
23	Marta likes taking photos when she's on holiday.	☐	☐
24	Jim's mother reads a lot when they go on holiday.	☐	☐
25	Marta is worried that her parents will be very serious on holiday.	☐	☐

Part 1

General conversation: saying who you are, spelling your name, giving personal information.

Take turns to be the examiner. Ask your partner questions to find out some information about each other.

Ask each other:
- What's your name?
- What's your surname?

- How do you spell it?
- Where do you come from?
- Are you a student or do you work?
- What do you do/study?
- How do you spend your day at the weekend?
- What do you enjoy about learning English?

Part 2

Simulated discussion: exchanging opinions, saying what is necessary.

Your examiner gives you both a picture. You do a task together.

A friend of yours is going to the UK to study for six months. Look at page 175. Talk about the different things your friend could take. Decide together which are the most important things for your friend to take.

Ask and answer questions like these:
- Do you think X will be useful?
- How often do you think our friend would use this?
- Which of these two would be more useful?
- Which things do you consider to be most important?
- Do you agree that X wouldn't be very important for our friend?

Part 3

You take turns to tell each other about a photograph.

Candidate A: Look at Photograph 3A on page 182.
Candidate B: Look at Photograph 3B on page 186.

Think about your photograph for a few seconds.
Describe it to your partner for about one minute.

Tell your partner about these things:
* who is in the picture
* what different people are doing in the picture
* where the people are
* how you think the people are feeling
* what you think is nice about the picture.

Part 4

General conversation about the photographs: talking about children.

The examiner asks you to talk to your partner.

Talk to each other about ways of looking after young children.

Use these ideas:
* Say whether many parents these days have to work all day.
* Talk about the best way to look after children during the day.
* Say how you would like to bring up your own children.
* Say what children like doing best.
* Talk about what is important for young children.

Reading

Part 1

Questions 1–5

Look at the text in each question.
What does it say?
Mark the correct letter **A**, **B** or **C** on your answer sheet.

Example:

0

> Charlie,
> Please can you pick up my coat from the dry cleaner's when you collect your suit? I'll give you the money this afternoon if that's OK.
> Thanks a lot!
> Vera

What will Charlie do?

A   Get paid back by Vera for the dry cleaning later today.

B   Take his clothes to the dry cleaner's.

C   Fetch Vera's suit from the dry cleaner's.

Answer:

1

> Pete,
> Rick rang and said don't take the A10 to London — there's been an accident and you'll be late for the match. Go on the A15 instead.
> Gina X

A   Pete needs to change route to arrive earlier.

B   Gina will come to the match if there's enough time.

C   Rick suggests taking the A10 to save time.

2

> To | Andre
> From | Ali
>
> Martina's coming next weekend so we're hiring a river boat. Do you want to join us? We need you to translate and you could help cook!

What does Ali want Andre to do?

A   Make all the meals on holiday.

B   Help everybody communicate.

C   Find a good river boat to hire.

3

GOODLIFE FITNESS CLUB
SPECIAL OFFER FOR EXISTING MEMBERS:
INTRODUCE A FRIEND TO THE CLUB AND
RECEIVE FREE SPORTS CLOTHES!
YOUR FRIEND MUST PAY 12-MONTH FEE.

A   You must pay your 12-month membership fee for Goodlife now.

B   Goodlife is selling sports clothes to members at special prices.

C   You can get a gift if you persuade a friend to join Goodlife.

4

Shen,
Doug told me Lina's doing a concert on Saturday. He might be able to get us tickets so let him know if you want to see her play.
Kim

Who should Shen contact if she wants to see the concert?

A   Kim.

B   Lina.

C   Doug.

5

To be taken between meals at four-hourly intervals, up to four times daily.

If taking this medicine, you must

A   eat just before you take it.

B   take it at least four times a day.

C   wait four hours before taking it again.

Part 2

Questions 6–10

The people below all want to visit a music website.
On the opposite page, there are reviews of eight music websites.
Decide which website would be most suitable for the following people.
For questions **6–10**, mark the correct letter (**A–H**) on your answer sheet.

6  Ravi is interested in a wide range of musical styles, although his favourite is African dance music. He doesn't have much money to spend on buying music for himself but likes giving CDs as presents.

7  Leila is very keen on dance music from the 1950s and 1960s, although she knows this kind of music is hard to find and expensive to buy.

8  Takumi enjoys going to concerts of various types of music, although he finds that tickets are very expensive. He likes giving CDs as presents to friends.

9  Ijeoma likes to listen to music while she's studying. She would like to work in the music industry in future. She buys CDs as often as she can afford it.

10  Wasim studies music at university. He goes to traditional and modern dance performances when he can afford to. He listens to music when he is running in the park.

Music sites on the web

A This is a very useful website and I certainly recommend it to music lovers with a taste for the tunes and songs of the dance halls in the middle of the last century. If you're looking for something that's not available elsewhere, or if you'd like to listen to parts of those old favourites for free, try here.

B This music website caters to all tastes. From early jazz through 1970s pop to current world music, you should be able to buy what you want here. Many songs are available to listen to for free, and there are some reasonably priced CDs, with an efficient present-ordering service.

C If you're hungry for live music, this is probably the best site for you. There's a comprehensive guide to all concerts every night, from the large classical shows to the small upstairs blues rooms. What's more, there are plenty of discounts to be had, from half-price entrance to shows to 10 percent off their express CD order line.

D This site says it's by musicians for musicians, with a focus on current dance music. There are lots of requests for new musicians to join new bands, and there are advertisements for performances, but the information is sometimes a little out of date. Worth a look, though.

E This interesting site is packed with information about all kinds of music, including articles about finding a job in the music business. As well as selling a good range of CDs at fair prices, they also offer a playlist facility, so you can put together hours of free listening to download.

F This is an unusual site, and will be just right for you if dance is what you like. You can save money with cheap tickets to see old and new ballet. There's a playlist facility which you can link to your MP3 player and there are articles about ballet's history, although these are a bit serious.

G This is an unusual site, and will be just right for you if dance is what you like. You can save money with cheap tickets to see old and new ballet. There's a playlist facility which you can link to your MP3 player and there are articles about ballet's history, although these are a bit serious.

H This site claims it can find you any ticket for any dance performance, although this service doesn't come cheap. They also claim they can find any CD ever recorded, though this claim may be harder to prove. Either way, they're great, but far from cheap.

Part 3

Look at the sentences below about what there is to do and see in a town.
Read the text on the opposite page to decide if each sentence is correct or incorrect.
If it is correct, mark **A** on your answer sheet.
If it is not correct, mark **B** on your answer sheet.

---

11 A paper called *What's On* is given free to homes and hotels in Heltonbrook.

12 There will soon be two new hotels in Heltonbrook to provide for growing numbers of visitors.

13 The Sports Day has taken place every year in Heltonbrook.

14 A local champion will help decide who wins sports events.

15 You must apply before the 12 July if you want to take part in the Sports Day.

16 Almost a thousand pictures will be for sale at no more than £800.

17 You can vote for your favourite picture at the Arts Show.

18 Open Spaces starts earlier than the other events this summer in Heltonbrook.

19 There will be more locations included than ever before, in this year's Open Spaces.

20 You should check to see if there are limits about visiting certain places in Open Spaces.

Heltonbrook Life:
What's on this summer

Search

[   ] GO

Hi! Welcome to your very own Heltonbrook *What's On* webpage! This is the place to find out what's going on around the town.

We hope you find this site useful. It was started two months ago, in response to requests from the public. We feel it is more environmentally responsible than the paper magazine we used to deliver free to houses, hotels and so on.

Heltonbrook is a small, but lively and popular town, with lots to offer both people who live here and the many visitors we are pleased to receive every year. With visitor numbers on the rise, a new hotel is being built near the centre, and the old Market Hotel is building 20 new rooms.

Sports Day

14 July will see Heltonbrook's first Sports Day, something we hope will become a regular feature in the town's calendar. There will be all sorts of sporting events and some great prizes to be won. Judges will include Greg Davids, our neighbourhood Olympic gold medallist, and Tim Progue, Head Teacher at Northfields School, and they will be giving our very own Heltonbrook medals to the winners of events as varied as 1,500 metres running, horse-riding skills, high diving … the list is a long one! For details on how to enter, click here or phone 01991 45451. Please note the closing date is 11 July.

Arts Show

The Heltonbrook Arts Show is rightly famous in our region, where it is the biggest temporary collection of art, with over 3,000 works of art by 800 artists. But what's really special about it is the prices: all the art is affordable, with pictures limited to £999, so this is your chance to take something home with you on the day. There will be an election – open to all who attend the Show – to decide the single best picture of all. The Show is open 10 a.m.–4 p.m., 15–18 July.

Open Spaces

This special feature of Heltonbrook life runs for a week, from 11–17 July. All sorts of hidden spaces are opened to the public, giving residents and visitors alike the chance to see what they normally can't. Beautiful gardens, ancient buildings, an old library in the college, the inside of the original prison building … each year a few more places are added to the list of Open Spaces. See the special programme for details of individual spaces and their opening hours, etc., and please note that there may be special conditions for some locations, such as no wheelchair access, for example, owing to their construction.

Part 4

Questions 21–25

Read the text and questions below.
For each question, mark the correct letter **A**, **B**, **C** or **D** on your answer sheet.

Learning about Learning Languages

In many ways, my interest in the whole business of language learning began with my grandmother. She was an immigrant and, as a young child going to school and having friends on the street, I was always confused that my grandmother spoke one language to me, another to my parents and a third one to my grandfather and on the phone to relatives back home. I guess she could have been a translator of books, or even a writer, as she seemed to pick languages up so quickly, but the amazing thing was that she'd left school at the age of 11 and had taught herself everything she knew.

The main reason to speak different languages for her was so she could communicate in these different cultures. She usually found out more about the people she was talking to than they did about her! Although it's often said that learning languages can help you to find higher-paid employment, these days, travel and the internet are generally happening in a kind of limited global English or can be translated electronically, so my grandmother has still got it right.

If she did, so can we. In fact, there's a lot of extra help these days from IT. Recording your voice with feedback facilities on web learning sites helps you to control how you speak, and so improve. I still think going to class means you can interact with other, real people in the same space, but it can also mean that you keep repeating the same mistakes. It's good to combine these methods. If you do a course, go for a full-time, intensive course.

Or you can just spend a little time chatting with my grandmother.

21 What is the writer's main purpose in writing the text?

   A   To explain which is the best way to learn a language.

   B   To describe different ways of learning languages.

   C   To encourage people to study harder when learning a language.

   D   To request information about learning different languages.

22 What does the writer think is special about her grandmother?

    A She spoke three languages.

    B She translated books for publishers.

    C She learnt languages without having teachers.

    D She could write quickly in different languages.

23 The writer says the most important reason why people use languages is

    A to learn about other cultures.

    B to travel internationally.

    C to get better jobs.

    D to use the internet.

24 The writer says IT helps you to learn languages because it means

    A you can study in different places.

    B you can talk to other learners.

    C you can repeat things easily.

    D you can check your mistakes.

25 What would the writer say to one of her friends?

    A I went to a language school today to join a part-time course, which I'm really looking forward to.

    B I'm really enjoying learning this new language because I'm mixing different ways of studying.

    C I've found a useful website where I can chat to other people about their ideas for learning languages.

    D I bought a big new dictionary today to help me with a translation job that I'm trying to finish.

Part 5

Read the text below and choose the correct word for each space.
For each question, mark the correct letter **A**, **B**, **C** or **D** on your answer sheet.

Example:

0 **A** for **B** by **C** with **D** in

Answer:

0	A	B	C	D
	■	☐	☐	☐

Rice

Rice has been an important food in Asia and Africa **(0)** ………… over 3,000 years. Farmers can **(26)** ………… several crops of rice in a single year, and rice is quite cheap to grow. **(27)** ………… days, rice is grown in many different countries.

It is a basic **(28)** ………… of the diet of billions of people on earth. Poor people may have rice **(29)** ………… for their meal, while others may eat it with vegetables, fish or meat. You can **(30)** ………… uncooked rice for a long time, **(31)** ………… it's useful for people who don't have fridges.

Rice is usually **(32)** ………… in water – everyone has a special **(33)** ………… of cooking it. Some people **(34)** ………… the rice while they cook it, for example, and others say you mustn't **(35)** ………… it when it is cooking.

26	**A** produce	**B** design	**C** invent	**D** discover
27	**A** Some	**B** These	**C** Most	**D** Those
28	**A** step	**B** row	**C** point	**D** part
29	**A** just	**B** separately	**C** alone	**D** exactly
30	**A** continue	**B** stay	**C** keep	**D** put
31	**A** since	**B** so	**C** because	**D** as
32	**A** grilled	**B** boiled	**C** roast	**D** baked
33	**A** way	**B** kind	**C** type	**D** sort
34	**A** push	**B** knock	**C** rock	**D** stir
35	**A** place	**B** contact	**C** touch	**D** stick

Writing

Part 1

Questions 1–5

Here are some sentences about a swimming class.
For each question, complete the second sentence so that it means the same as the first.
Use no more than three words.
Write only the missing words on your answer sheet.
You may use this page for any rough work.

Example:

0   Hilda and Sally first became keen on swimming when they were very young.

Hilda and Sally .... **keen on swimming since they were very young.**

Answer:

0	have been

---

1   Last month, Sally suggested joining a swimming class together.

Last month, Sally said, 'Why .... **join a swimming class together?'**

2   It was the first swimming class they had attended.

They .... **a swimming class before.**

3   It was such an enjoyable class they decided to go every week.

The class was .... **enjoyable they decided to go every week.**

4   They realise they won't get better if they don't practise.

They realise they won't get better .... **they practise.**

5   They both like the sea more than the pool.

They both prefer the sea .... **the pool.**

Part 2

Question 6

You want to borrow your friend's bike.

Write an email to your friend. In your email, you should

- ask to borrow your friend's bike

- explain why you want to borrow the bike

- offer to do something to say thank you.

Write **35–45 words** on your answer sheet.

Part 3

Write an answer to **one** of the questions (**7** or **8**) in this part.
Write your answer in about **100 words** on your answer sheet.
Mark the question number in the box at the top of your answer sheet.

Question 7

- This is part of a letter you receive from an English friend, Jane.

> My favourite subject at school is history. I don't like science. What subjects do you study? What's your favourite, and what subjects don't you like?

- Now write a letter to Jane, answering her questions.

- Write your **letter** in about 100 words on your answer sheet.

Question 8

- Your English teacher has asked you to write a story.

- Your story must have the following title:

A new boy arrives at school

- Write your **story** in about 100 words on your answer sheet.

Part 1

Questions 1–7

There are seven questions in this part.
For each question, there are three pictures and a short recording.
Choose the correct picture and put a tick (✓) in the box below it.

Example: Which are Sara's cousins?

A ✓   B ☐   C ☐

---

1   Where does the girl want to go at the weekend?

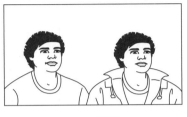  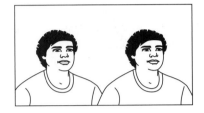

A ☐   B ☐   C ☐

2   When will Dan have his party?

  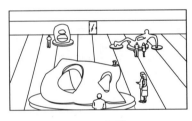

A ☐   B ☐   C ☐

3   Which photo does the woman like most?

A ☐   B ☐   C ☐

4 What will be on TV at 9 p.m.?

A ☐

B ☐

C ☐

5 What do they decide to buy Ivan for his birthday?

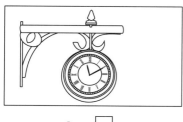

A ☐

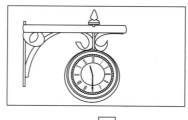

B ☐

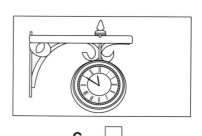

C ☐

6 What time does the last bus leave?

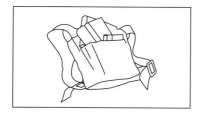

A ☐

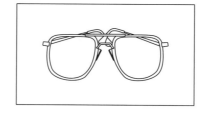

B ☐

C ☐

7 What is the weather like today?

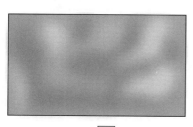

A ☐

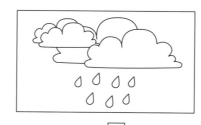

B ☐

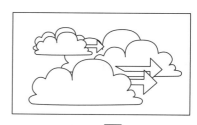

C ☐

Part 2

Questions 8–13

You will hear a man giving a talk about a steam railway.
For each question, put a tick (✓) in the correct box.

8   The speaker became interested in steam
trains when

    A   he was at university. ☐

    B   he visited his grandfather. ☐

    C   he was given a toy train. ☐

9   What does he currently do?

    A   He acts as chairman of the Steam Railways Club. ☐

    B   He runs the Steam Railways Club website. ☐

    C   He teaches train driving for the
Steam Railways Club. ☐

10   When did the original steam railway line close?

    A   1948 ☐

    B   1964 ☐

    C   1969 ☐

11   When did the Steam Railways Club take
its first passengers?

    A   1985 ☐

    B   1990 ☐

    C   1993 ☐

12   What will the Club introduce next?

    A   Educational visits for schools. ☐

    B   Tickets to travel in the driver's compartment. ☐

    C   Meals on the trains during journeys. ☐

13   What does the speaker think is most
important about the Club?

    A   Preserving trains and stations. ☐

    B   Making children interested in transport. ☐

    C   Bringing history to life. ☐

Part 3

Questions 14–19

You will hear a woman talking about holiday jobs for students.
For each question, fill in the missing information in the numbered space.

Holiday Jobs

There's a wide range of holiday jobs available.

Most people decide to do a holiday job to get
(14) ....

The best way to get information is from some
(15) ....

When writing about a possible job, make sure your letter is
(16) ....

Prepare carefully for the (17) ....

Think carefully about what (18) .... are
involved in a job.

Probably avoid jobs which are in the (19) ....

Part 4

Questions 20–25

Look at the six sentences for this part.
You will hear a man who works in a shop talking to a customer.
Decide if each sentence is correct or incorrect.
If it is correct, put a tick (✓) in the box under **A** for **YES**.
If it is not correct, put a tick (✓) in the box under **B** for **NO**.

		A YES	B NO
20	The shop was recommended to the customer by a friend of hers.	☐	☐
21	The man has worked in the shop for several years.	☐	☐
22	The customer wants to buy a jacket as a present to give her sister.	☐	☐
23	The customer prefers leather jackets generally.	☐	☐
24	The man is expecting some new jackets soon.	☐	☐
25	The man can reduce the price of the jacket that the customer wants.	☐	☐

Part 1

General conversation: saying who you are, spelling your name, giving personal information.

Take turns to be the examiner. Ask your partner questions to find out some information about each other.

Ask each other:
- What's your name?
- What's your surname?

- How do you spell it?
- Where do you come from?
- Are you a student or do you work?
- What do you do/study?
- What did you do yesterday evening?
- Where would you like to go during your next holiday?

Part 2

Simulated discussion: exchanging opinions, saying what is necessary.

Your examiner gives you both a picture. You do a task together.

A family are going to spend the weekend together. Look at page 176. Talk about the different things the family members could do. Decide together which ones would be most enjoyable for the family.

Ask and answer questions like these:
- Do you think everyone would like this?
- Which people would like this one?
- Would everyone be able to talk together here?
- If we chose just one, which one would be best for the family?
- Maybe this one isn't such a good idea?

Part 3

Responding to photographs: describing what people are doing and how they are feeling.

You take turns to tell each other about a photograph.

Candidate A: Look at Photograph 4A on page 182.
Candidate B: Look at Photograph 4B on page 186.

Think about your photograph for a few seconds.
Describe it to your partner for about one minute.

Tell your partner about these things:
- what you can see in the picture
- who is in the picture
- what you like about the picture
- how the person or people are feeling.

Part 4

General conversation about the photographs: talking about preferences and places to live.

The examiner asks you to talk to your partner.

Talk to each other about different places to live in.

Use these ideas:
- Say what kind of house or flat you live in.
- Talk about what homes people have in cities.
- Talk about the home you would most like to have.
- Say why some people prefer to live in the countryside.

Reading

Part 1

Questions 1–5

Look at the text in each question.
What does it say?
Mark the correct letter **A**, **B** or **C** on your answer sheet.

Example:

0

> Charlie,
> Please can you pick up my coat from the dry cleaner's when you collect your suit? I'll give you the money this afternoon if that's OK. Thanks a lot!
> Vera

What will Charlie do?

A Get paid back by Vera for the dry cleaning later today.

B Take his clothes to the dry cleaner's.

C Fetch Vera's suit from the dry cleaner's.

Answer:

0	A	B	C

1

NARROW TUNNEL

CYCLISTS – LEAVE ROAD AND JOIN PAVEMENT, BUT LOOK OUT FOR PEDESTRIANS!

A This tunnel is for cyclists and pedestrians only.

B Car drivers should look out for cyclists and pedestrians in the road.

C Pedestrians and cyclists should go through the tunnel on the pavement.

2

> Debbie,
> Brian's decided to attend the advanced guitar class and not the intermediate, and hopes you will too. Please let him know. It starts immediately after the intermediate class.
> Vickie

A Brian wants Debbie to go to the same guitar class as him.

B Debbie should tell Brian the exact time his guitar class starts.

C Brian is asking to join the advanced guitar class that Debbie teaches.

3

TONIGHT'S PERFORMANCE

This window is only for collecting tickets you have paid for.

A This window is only for collecting tickets you have reserved.

B Remaining tickets for tonight's performance are on sale at this window.

C There are no more tickets available for tonight's performance.

4

Hi Darragh,

I hear you've got a problem with homework. Would you like me to come round so we can talk about it?

Hannah

A Hannah is asking Darragh to help her with a problem.

B Hannah is offering to help Darragh with a problem.

C Hannah is advising Darragh about how to solve a problem.

5

SIGNAL PROBLEMS
All trains are running late,
many are cancelled. Details
from ticket office.

A Because of signal problems, it is impossible to travel by train at the moment.

B Passengers should enquire in the ticket office whether the train they want is running.

C The ticket office is currently unable to provide information about the times of trains.

Part 2

Questions 6–10

The people below are all looking for somewhere to eat.
On the opposite page, there are advertisements for eight restaurants and cafés.
Decide which restaurant or café would be most suitable for the following people.
For questions **6–10**, mark the correct letter (**A–H**) on your answer sheet.

---

6  Juan is going to the cinema in the city centre, and needs to eat after he finishes work at 5.30 p.m. He will have no more than an hour to eat. He loves steak.

7  Annie and Steve are going out for lunch to celebrate their wedding anniversary. They particularly like fish, and want to go to a restaurant in an old building outside the city.

8  Hasan and some British friends are meeting at the stadium for an afternoon football match. He wants to introduce them to Middle-Eastern food before the match starts. They are students, and can't afford much.

9  Tomiko and her friend Mafumi are visiting the city on Sunday, and want to try some African food before they go to the art gallery in the afternoon.

10  Ebele has just finished college and her parents want to take her out on Saturday evening for a special dinner in the city centre. Ebele would prefer a restaurant that only serves vegetarian food.

Places to eat in and around the city

A New Day

Since we opened 40 years ago, thousands of people have come to taste what the Middle East has to offer. We're not far from the stadium, and on bus routes from the city centre. You'll be surprised how little a good meal can cost! Open 9 a.m. till 4 p.m. every day.

B Buckden's

Close to the art gallery, Buckden's offers wonderful steak, at a price you can afford! Tell us if you're in a hurry, and we'll serve you quickly. Open 12.30 – 5.30 p.m., Monday to Saturday.

C The Red House

Whether or not it's a special occasion, come to The Red House. Situated in a seventeenth-century farmhouse in an attractive village within easy reach of the city, we've been open since 1990 and are famous for our fish and vegetarian dishes. Open seven days a week, noon until midnight.

D Flamingo

Right in the heart of the city, beside the art gallery, Flamingo is the ideal vegetarian restaurant for a meal to remember. Our food is based on African recipes. Come for something quick before an evening out, or spend the evening with us. Open every day, except Sunday, 11 a.m. to 11 p.m.

E Peggotty's

Just a short walk from the stadium, Peggotty's is a fish restaurant with a difference. Open every evening, we have live music and a great atmosphere. Our prices are very reasonable, and if you eat with us this month we'll give you a dessert absolutely free!

F The Bridge

Eat at The Bridge and you'll want to come back soon – our customers say our steaks are the best in the world! And if you're short of time, don't worry – we'll make sure you leave when you need to. We're right in the centre of the city, and are open from midday until late, seven days a week.

G Riverside

For an affordable meal in a beautiful countryside location, come to Riverside. We serve traditional food, and currently have a special offer on steaks – two meals for the price of one! We're open every evening from Wednesday to Sunday.

H The Crocus

If you're looking for something special, look no further! Our menu offers you the best in food from all over Africa – meat, fish and vegetarian. The Crocus is close to the city art gallery and is open for lunch seven days a week.

Part 3

Look at the sentences below about foreign language courses at a college in the UK.
Read the text on the opposite page to decide if each sentence is correct or incorrect.
If it is correct, mark **A** on your answer sheet.
If it is not correct, mark **B** on your answer sheet.

---

11   The college has recently increased the number of languages that students can study.

12   The language with the largest number of students last year was French.

13   Students must have some knowledge of certain languages before they take a course in them.

14   There may be a limit on which languages a student can study at the same time.

15   All interpreting and translation courses include English as one of the two languages.

16   Students must spend a period living abroad.

17   The college will rent an accommodation facility for students who go abroad to study.

18   Most teachers of translation and interpreting courses speak English as their first language.

19   The courses are mainly for students who use a foreign language in their work.

20   The college can put students in contact with possible employers.

Foreign Language Courses at Saville Language College

What can you study?

If you're interested in learning a foreign language, Saville College is the ideal place! We offer part-time courses in over 25 foreign languages, from Hindi to Zulu, Guaraní to Bulgarian. This year we are offering a record number of languages, with the addition of Greenlandish, Farsi and Catalan. European languages are generally the most popular courses, although last year, Mandarin Chinese overtook French to attract the largest number of students.

You can take a beginners' course in any language, and, in addition, we offer intermediate and advanced courses in Arabic, Spanish, Japanese and many other languages. You can study two or three languages at the same time, though please remember that the demands of the timetable may make certain choices impossible. Classes are mostly taught in the language you are studying, with as little English as possible.

What does a course include?

Every language course covers the four skills of speaking, listening, reading and writing, together with the history and culture of the country or countries where the language is spoken. We also offer courses in interpreting and translation between certain languages and English.

We firmly believe that it's extremely useful to spend a few months in a country where the language is spoken. So if you can, we encourage you to do this. We will arrange for you to attend a language course in that country, and advise you about ways of finding accommodation. You will then need to make your own arrangements.

Who are our trainers?

All our trainers are qualified teachers, translators or interpreters. Most of them speak the language they teach as their first language, as well as being fluent speakers of English.

How can our courses help you?

People study foreign languages for many reasons. Some, purely for pleasure. Others, because they want to go to another country on holiday or to live. Yet others learn because they intend to use the language in their work – perhaps to do business with another country, or to translate literature into English. Whatever your reason, you'll find that our courses are designed with your needs in mind.

However, if you're looking for a job, Saville can set up meetings for you with businesses that need your skills. Several major organisations come to us first when they're looking for new employees with foreign language skills.

So why not find out more about how you can benefit from taking a course at Saville Language College? Contact us **now** – it might be the best move you ever make!

Part 4

Questions 21–25

Read the text and questions below.
For each question, mark the correct letter **A**, **B**, **C** or **D** on your answer sheet.

Clevedon Drama Club – A Way of Life

by Warren Jackson

I've always lived in Clevedon. Both my parents love the theatre, and my father writes plays in his spare time. He keeps sending them to publishers, and though they always come back with a polite note saying 'No, thank you', he never gives up. Still, a few drama clubs have performed his plays, so my first visit to the theatre was to see one of my father's. Being only eight, I was too young to understand it, so although I enjoyed myself, I didn't go back to the theatre for years.

When I was 16, Clevedon Drama Club produced one of my father's plays, but a week before the first night, they had a problem: the lighting designer fell ill. Nobody else in the club could take over, and my father asked me. I didn't really have time – because of schoolwork – or knowledge, but I can never say no to a challenge, so I agreed.

As with the rest of the production team – the people doing scenery, costumes, and so on – it took a lot of hard work before the performance, but I certainly learned what a difference good lighting can make. It can attract the audience's attention to a certain spot, it can suggest danger, it can make the audience feel cheerful or relaxed. I found that very exciting! And a lot of people said the lighting was excellent!

That was just the beginning. I've been a member ever since, and designed the lighting, painted scenery or sold programmes. Our next production will be my tenth with the club – but I'll be appearing on stage for the first time!

21 What is Warren trying to do in the text?

   A Explain why he joined the club.

   B Describe the history of the club.

   C Encourage people to help the club.

   D Advertise the club's next production.

22 Warren says that his father

    A was a full-time writer.

    B had some of his plays published.

    C failed to achieve his ambitions as a writer.

    D was sometimes disappointed with performances of his plays.

23 Why did Warren get involved with Clevedon Drama Club?

    A He wanted to learn how to do stage lighting.

    B He agreed to a request for help.

    C He wanted a change from his schoolwork.

    D He thought he could do the lighting well.

24 What does Warren say he enjoyed about doing the lighting?

    A Being in the production team.

    B Planning it before the performance.

    C Creating an atmosphere.

    D Explaining what he was doing.

25 Which of these is the best description of Warren?

A

> He puts a lot of effort into activities that he enjoys, and likes to try something new so he can develop additional skills.

B

> He has been keen on the theatre ever since he was a child, and would love to have a career in the theatre.

C

> He and his father have similar interests, and they are planning to work together on drama productions in the future.

D

> He thinks that drama is a good hobby because it is very different from school and other activities.

Part 5

Questions 26–35

Read the text below and choose the correct word for each space.
For each question, mark the correct letter **A**, **B**, **C** or **D** on your answer sheet.

Example:

0	**A** long	**B** wide	**C** deep	**D** broad

Answer:

0	**A** ▆	**B** ☐	**C** ☐	**D** ☐

Bird-watching

The relationship between birds and human beings goes back a very **(0)** .... way – in fact, for thousands of years. Birds have always **(26)** .... us with food, but people have only been **(27)** .... in bird-watching since the late 1700s. In the following century, the **(28)** .... of birds became popular, although in those days it really only **(29)** .... collecting birds' eggs. Rich collectors often **(30)** .... use of their contacts in other countries, **(31)** .... for eggs and birds to be sent to them. **(32)** .... the end of the century, people began to realise that birds needed protection. Many people now watched living birds, helped by cheaper equipment for watching them at a distance.

As cars became more common, increasing **(33)** .... of bird-watchers started travelling from place to place **(34)** .... the country to see birds that were unknown in their own area. And in the 1960s, cheap air travel **(35)** .... people to go abroad to watch birds.

26	**A** provided	**B** given	**C** offered	**D** delivered
27	**A** curious	**B** fond	**C** keen	**D** interested
28	**A** search	**B** study	**C** exploration	**D** enquiry
29	**A** contained	**B** added	**C** involved	**D** included
30	**A** made	**B** brought	**C** kept	**D** took
31	**A** requesting	**B** insisting	**C** asking	**D** demanding
32	**A** Towards	**B** Into	**C** Through	**D** Over
33	**A** quantities	**B** amounts	**C** totals	**D** numbers
34	**A** against	**B** between	**C** around	**D** beside
35	**A** confirmed	**B** encouraged	**C** promised	**D** excited

Writing

Part 1

Questions 1–5

Here are some sentences about surfing.
For each question, complete the second sentence so that it means the same as the first.
Use no more than three words.
Write only the missing words on your answer sheet.
You may use this page for any rough work.

Example:

0   My brother has just become a London bus driver.

     My brother recently .... a London bus driver.

Answer:
0	became

---

1   He's very careful when he drives, so he doesn't have an accident.

     He drives very .... , to avoid having an accident.

2   He thinks it's more fun to drive a bus than a car.

     He enjoys .... a bus more than a car.

3   Passengers say other drivers don't help them as much as he does.

     Passengers say he is .... other drivers.

4   There aren't enough bus drivers in London.

     There are too .... bus drivers in London.

5   In my opinion, he's the best driver of all.

     In my opinion, none of the other drivers are .... he is.

Part 2

Question 6

Your English friend, Sally, who lives in your country, has invited you to spend a day at her home.

Write an email to Sally. In your email you should

- accept her invitation

- suggest something you would like to do

- ask her for directions.

Write **35–45 words** on your answer sheet.

Part 3

Write an answer to **one** of the questions (**7** or **8**) in this part.
Write your answer in about **100 words** on your answer sheet.
Mark the question number in the box at the top of your answer sheet.

Question 7

- This is part of a letter you receive from your American friend, Jerry.

> My family and I are going to your country next summer for a two-week holiday. What places should we visit? What is the best way to travel around?

- Now write a letter to Jerry, answering his questions.

- Write your **letter** in about 100 words on your answer sheet.

Question 8

- Your English teacher has asked you to write a story.

- Your story must have this title:

I was visiting a town for the first time when someone called out my name

- Write your **story** in about 100 words on your answer sheet.

Part 1

Questions 1–7

There are seven questions in this part.
For each question, there are three pictures and a short recording.
Choose the correct picture and put a tick (✔) in the box below it.

Example: Which are Sara's cousins?

A ✔

B ☐

C ☐

---

1 What will the weather be like tomorrow?

A ☐

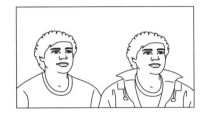

B ☐

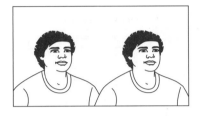

C ☐

2 What class does Jessica decide to join?

A ☐

B ☐

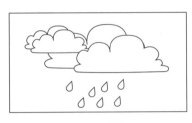

C ☐

3 What time did the man arrive home yesterday?

A ☐

B ☐

C ☐

4 Which is the woman's flat?

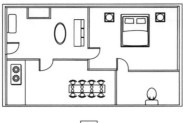

A ☐

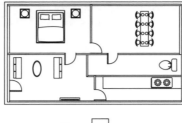

B ☐

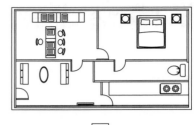

C ☐

5 Where does Jill want Sally to go to?

A ☐

B ☐

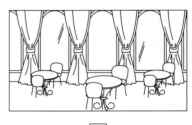

C ☐

6 Which photograph are they looking at?

A ☐

B ☐

C ☐

7 Where did the customer leave her glasses?

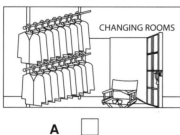

A ☐

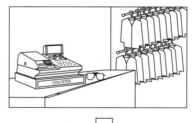

B ☐

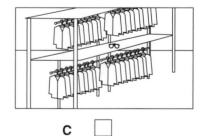

C ☐

Part 2

Questions 8–13

You will hear a man on the radio reviewing last weekend's television programmes.
For each question, put a tick (✓) in the correct box.

8 What does the reviewer say about *Street Dancing*?

   A It started late. ☐

   B It was cancelled. ☐

   C It was shorter than usual. ☐

9 What did the reviewer particularly like about *Plants of Australia*?

   A It was beautiful to look at. ☐

   B It gave a lot of information. ☐

   C It was filmed in unusual locations. ☐

10 The reviewer says the series *Jojo's party*

   A ended at the weekend. ☐

   B will continue until October. ☐

   C started six months ago. ☐

11 *Who knows?* was different from usual because it

   A was mostly about sport. ☐

   B had a new group of experts. ☐

   C included questions from the audience. ☐

12 The reviewer thinks that Sunday's *Police Officer Briggs* was

   A surprisingly good. ☐

   B the worst in the series. ☐

   C of its usual standard. ☐

13 Vanessa Cosgrave wasn't in *It's Comedy Time!* on Sunday because

   A she was away on holiday. ☐

   B she arrived late at the studio. ☐

   C she has left the programme. ☐

Questions 14–19

You will hear a holiday representative talking to some new guests at their hotel.
For each question, fill in the missing information in the numbered space.

Greville Weston Tours

Holiday representative: Cathy

This week's programme

Tomorrow: Free

Monday evening: Barbecue beside the (14) ....
Entertainment by teenage (15) ....
Starts at 8 p.m.
Sign the list before (16) .... on Monday.

Wednesday morning: Coach trip to the (17) ....
that can be seen in the distance.
Take a (18) ....
Coach leaves at 9 a.m., returns around 4 p.m.
Cost of (19) .... is included.

Part 4

Questions 20–25

Look at the six sentences for this part.
You will hear a girl, Alice and a boy, Tom, talking about their school.
Decide if each sentence is correct or incorrect.
If it is correct, put a tick (✓) in the box under **A** for **YES**.
If it is not correct, put a tick (✓) in the box under **B** for **NO**.

		A YES	B NO
20	Tom started at the school because his family moved.	☐	☐
21	Alice thinks that it is the best school in the city.	☐	☐
22	Tom can join the orchestra that Alice plays in.	☐	☐
23	Tom enjoys music classes most of all.	☐	☐
24	Tom thinks there are too many sports classes.	☐	☐
25	Alice is looking forward to her next lesson.	☐	☐

Part 1

General conversation: saying who you are, spelling your name, giving personal information.

Take turns to be the examiner. Ask your partner questions to find out some information about each other.

Ask each other at least four of these questions:
- What's your name?
- What's your surname?
- How do you spell it?
- Where do you come from?
- Are you a student or do you work?
- What do you do/study?
- Do you live in a city, a village or somewhere else?
- How long will you continue to study English?

Part 2

Simulated situation: exchanging opinions, saying what you think is necessary.

Your examiner gives you both a picture. You do a task together.

You are going to travel together on a flight that takes about 14 hours. Look at page 177. There are some ideas of things you could take. Talk together about what you can do during the flight, and decide which are the best things to take with you.

Ask and answer questions like these:
- How much time will we spend eating or sleeping?
- What would take up most time?
- Do we want to do things together or separately?
- What would we enjoy doing?
- Would there be enough room?

Part 3

Responding to photographs: describing where people are and what they are doing.

You take turns to tell each other about a photograph.

Candidate A: Look at Photograph 5A on page 183.
Candidate B: Look at Photograph 5B on page 187.

Think about your photograph for a few seconds.
Describe it to your partner for about one minute.

Tell your partner about these things:
- where the people are
- what they are doing
- why they are there instead of somewhere else
- whether they look interested or bored
- what the student in the centre is thinking.

Part 4

General conversation about the photographs: talking about studying and preferences.

The examiner asks you to talk to your partner.
You give your opinion about something and
explain what you prefer.

Tell each other about different ways of studying.

Use these ideas:
- Say how much time you spend (or used to spend) studying outside class.
- Talk about whether you prefer studying alone or with other people.
- Say whether you think a computer is useful for studying.
- Say where you can study best, and why.
- Talk about what helps you to study.

Reading

Part 1

Questions 1–5

Look at the text in each question.
What does it say?
Mark the correct letter **A**, **B** or **C** on your answer sheet.

Example:

0

> Charlie,
> Please can you pick up my coat from the dry cleaner's when you collect your suit? I'll give you the money this afternoon if that's OK.
> Thanks a lot!
> Vera

What will Charlie do?

A Get paid back by Vera for the dry cleaning later today.

B Take his clothes to the dry cleaner's.

C Fetch Vera's suit from the dry cleaner's.

Answer:

0	A	B	C
	▬	☐	☐

1

> **Coach trip:**
> **No places available. If you've paid a deposit, final payment due tomorrow.**

Tomorrow is the last day for

A paying what you owe for the coach trip.

B saying you want to go on the coach trip.

C paying a deposit for the coach trip.

2

> Kelly,
> The library phoned. Three of the books you reserved have arrived and will be held for seven days. The others are expected next month.

A Kelly cannot collect any of the books she reserved until next month.

B Kelly can only keep the books she reserved for seven days.

C Kelly can now collect some of the books she reserved.

3

ONCE OPENED, THE MEDICINE IN THIS BOTTLE SHOULD BE CONSUMED WITHIN SIX MONTHS.

A You should drink the medicine in this bottle over a period of six months.

B You should drink the medicine no more than six months after opening the bottle.

C You should open this bottle within six months of buying it.

4

John,

I have to go out urgently, so I'm afraid you'll have to look after Belinda. Sorry you won't be able to go swimming after all.

Mum

This note asks John

A to take Belinda swimming with him.

B to go out with Mum instead of going swimming.

C to take care of Belinda instead of going swimming.

5

CHILDREN'S SCIENCE EXHIBITION

MACHINES HAVE BUTTONS WHICH SHOULD BE PRESSED TO MAKE THEM START.

A The machines are designed so that children can operate them.

B Children should be careful not to touch the machines.

C The machines are models which do not work.

Part 2

The people below are all looking for somewhere to go on holiday.
On the opposite page, there are advertisements for eight holidays organised by the same company.
Decide which holiday would be most suitable for the following people.
For questions **6–10**, mark the correct letter (**A–H**) on your answer sheet.

6

Maggie would like a holiday with other people in their twenties. She wants to go diving during the day, and go out dancing and to different restaurants every evening. She only has a week free.

7

Vicky and Alexia are interested in mountain climbing. They want to sleep in tents and make their own food, and to spend four or five weeks on their holiday.

8

Johannes lives in the countryside. He hopes to spend a few days in a big city, ideally in the home of somebody who can tell him about life in the city.

9

The Stefanovski family want to spend two or three weeks walking in the countryside. They would like to stay somewhere new each night, but don't want to have to carry their luggage.

10

Sonam and her parents want to go on holiday together for two weeks or longer. Sonam would like to explore different towns, but her parents would prefer to travel on a ship and relax on board.

Robson Clark Holidays

A Our guide leads a group of 12–15 people on a walk of around 15 kilometres a day, through some of the most beautiful countryside in Italy. Each day's walk takes you to a different hotel, where you'll find your luggage has already arrived. Choose between tours lasting two and four weeks.

B Join a group of mostly young people for a lively holiday in a small town on a Greek island. Spend the day swimming, diving or sailing in the beautiful blue sea. There are plenty of places to eat and dance. Book any number of weeks, from one to four.

C Spend two weeks in New Zealand. You'll be based in a family hotel, and our guide will lead walks through the amazing countryside with views of mountains in the distance. The hotel will provide picnic lunches, and there's dancing every evening!

D Cruise through the Great Lakes of North America and admire the wonderful scenery while you sit and relax on deck. Many of the towns where the ship calls have hardly changed for over a century. Each cruise lasts one week.

E We can help you to visit some of the amazing sights of Peru. We've planned a route and can advise on where to camp and where to buy food. We can also supply tents and the essential equipment for mountain climbing. We recommend at least three weeks for this trip.

F Enjoy 21 days on a luxury cruise ship travelling from Cape Town to London. The ship offers swimming pool, sports facilities, entertainment and five restaurants. And you can go ashore when it calls at ports along the coast of southern and West Africa.

G Do you enjoy camping? Then this is the holiday for you! Three weeks in Sri Lanka based in a number of campsites with excellent facilities, where you can cook your own food or sample the fare prepared by experienced chefs.

H Learn about Mexico from its inhabitants! You stay as the guest of a Mexican family for up to a week – choose between a city and the countryside. You eat with them and they'll show you the places they like.

Part 3

Questions 11–20

Look at the sentences below about the town of Huntingdon, in the UK.
Read the text on the opposite page to decide if each sentence is correct or incorrect.
If it is correct, mark **A** on your answer sheet.
If it is not correct, mark **B** on your answer sheet.

---

11 Huntingdon began to develop before the Romans controlled England.

12 The first castle in Huntingdon was built of stone.

13 The first castle was destroyed by the King of England.

14 Part of the castle can still be seen.

15 There were a lot of trees around Huntingdon in the twelfth century.

16 Huntingdon bought the right to hold a market from King John.

17 People came to Huntingdon from other places to sell goods in the market.

18 At the History Festival, you can find out about the clothes worn in the Middle Ages.

19 Free entry to the festival is limited to people who live in Huntingdon.

20 The organisers expect about the same number of visitors as at the 2005 festival.

HISTORY FESTIVAL IN HUNTINGDON

Huntingdon is a small town about 100 kilometres north of London. It is situated in a low-lying area beside the River Great Ouse, and the land was probably too wet for people to live there thousands of years ago. However, when the Romans ruled England, 2,000 years ago, they constructed many roads. One of them, Ermine Street, runs from London to York, in the north of England. People began to build homes where it crossed the Great Ouse. This became an important place, as it was possible to travel along both the river and the road. The first document to mention Huntingdon was written in the year AD 650.

Huntingdon's first castle dates from 1068, and while many castles of the Middle Ages were built of stone, this one was wooden. In 1174, King William of Scotland gained the title of Earl of Huntingdon, although Scotland and England were separate countries then. William came south with an army to his castle in Huntingdon, and fought against an English army. The English won, and the English king ordered that William's castle should be burnt down. Nothing now remains of that castle.

One of Huntingdon's inhabitants in the twelfth century wrote that the town was an attractive place, with beautiful buildings, including 16 churches. It had about 2,000 inhabitants and was fairly rich. It was surrounded by forests, providing wood for fuel, buildings and fences.

In 1205, King John confirmed Huntingdon's right to hold a weekly market. This was a common way that the kings of England in the Middle Ages raised money, as towns had to pay for the right – and King John was in serious need of money. The previous king, his brother Richard, had spent enormous sums on fighting wars.

Markets were the main place for trade in the Middle Ages, and the town was busy on the days when they were held. Huntingdon had several inns where visiting traders could stay overnight.

History Festival

To celebrate Huntingdon's rich history, the Town Council has arranged a History Festival for the weekend of 26–27 June, when you'll be able to step back in time and experience life in the Middle Ages. Among the many activities, you'll be able to learn dances and get advice about the fashions of the period. There will be a historical market, and local clubs and other organisations will have their own stalls.

There is no charge for admission to the festival, which is expected to attract thousands of people both from the town and from further away. The Council is aiming to repeat the success of the last festival it organised, in 2005, which attracted over 20,000 visitors.

Part 4

Read the text and questions below.
For each question, mark the correct letter **A**, **B**, **C** or **D** on your answer sheet.

An Early Expert on Plants and Animals

Jean-Baptiste Lamarck, a French expert on plants and animals, lived from 1744 to 1829. He was the eleventh child in a family that had a high position in French society, but was very poor. It was a tradition in the family that the sons joined the army, and several of Lamarck's older brothers did so. Following the death of his father, Lamarck also decided to follow his brothers. Aged only 16, he bought a horse and rode across the country to join the army.

While he was in the army, he read a book on botany – the study of plants – and became interested in the natural world. He studied botany, and soon became an expert on the subject. He later published a major study of the plants that grew in France, and this made him well known among French scientists. In 1781, he was made a royal botanist. As part of his work he travelled to botanical gardens in other countries, where he collected and took home plants that were not available in France.

In 1793, Lamarck became a professor of zoology – the study of animals. He developed the idea that different types of animals change over time, an idea that hardly anyone at that time believed. Half a century later, the scientist Charles Darwin also believed that living things change to fit their environment better. However, Darwin thought Lamarck was wrong about how these changes were caused, and he developed his own explanations.

Lamarck married three times, and all his wives died before him. When he died in 1829, his family was so poor that they had to ask for financial help.

21   In this text, the writer is describing

    A   how Lamarck balanced his career with his private life.

    B   the way that Lamarck achieved his objectives.

    C   why Lamarck kept losing his job.

    D   the range of Lamarck's interests.

22 What is said about Lamarck's family?

    A   It was one of the richest in France.

    B   He was the only boy in the family.

    C   Many family members joined the army.

    D   His father bought a horse for him.

23 One of Lamarck's activities in the 1780s was to

    A   bring back plants that could not be found in France.

    B   make French plants known in other countries.

    C   create botanical gardens in several countries.

    D   make the study of plants popular among scientists.

24 What does the writer say about Lamarck and Darwin?

    A   Darwin's work was only possible because of Lamarck's ideas.

    B   They gave different explanations of how changes in animals happen.

    C   Darwin did not know about Lamarck's work.

    D   They shared the opinions of most people of their time.

25 Which of these might Lamarck have written to a friend in 1829?

A

I am delighted that my success as a scientist has made me both rich and well known among world scientists.

B

I am satisfied that I have discovered a number of plants which have changed scientific understanding of plant life.

C

I am disappointed that the problems I have had throughout my life have led to my present difficult situation.

D

I am glad I have added to knowledge in more than one area of science, but new ideas will take the place of mine.

Part 5

Read the text below and choose the correct word for each space.
For each question, mark the correct letter **A**, **B**, **C** or **D** on your answer sheet.

Example:

0 **A** taught **B** showed **C** learnt **D** managed

Answer:

0	A	B	C	D
	■	☐	☐	☐

My Life in Books

It was my parents, of course, who **(0)** .... me
to read. I can't **(26)** .... my life before reading,
without books. When I started reading, a book was
mainly pictures. Now **(27)** .... I am older, a book
(28) .... only words in most cases. **(29)** ....
I also love art books, **(30)** .... the pages to look
slowly and hungrily at paintings **(31)** .... the
walls of galleries and museums around the planet.

I spend hours and hours reading, lost in other worlds, travelling, dreaming, imagining
people and places. Books **(32)** .... me smells and sounds I may never experience
directly, but **(33)** .... seem to make my life more interesting.

This love of books is not without **(34)** .... own problems. For example, when
I go to the cinema to watch a film with friends, I don't get as excited as they
(35) .... I can't wait to get back home to my books.

26	**A** repeat	**B** register	**C** remind	**D** remember
27	**A** then	**B** so	**C** that	**D** how
28	**A** counts	**B** controls	**C** keeps	**D** contains
29	**A** But	**B** Or	**C** And	**D** Why
30	**A** changing	**B** turning	**C** putting	**D** placing
31	**A** with	**B** in	**C** from	**D** at
32	**A** move	**B** carry	**C** bring	**D** pull
33	**A** who	**B** what	**C** where	**D** which
34	**A** its	**B** their	**C** the	**D** some
35	**A** be	**B** do	**C** make	**D** go

Writing

Part 1

Questions 1–5

Here are some sentences about joining an exercise class.
For each question, complete the second sentence so that it means the same as the first.
Use no more than three words.
Write only the missing words on your answer sheet.
You may use this page for any rough work.

Example:

0   My sister recently decided to join an exercise class.

My sister recently made the .... to join an exercise class.

Answer:

0	**decision**

---

1   She didn't want to go by herself.

She wasn't keen .... by herself.

2   She asked me to go to the class with her.

She asked if I .... to the class with her.

3   At the fitness centre the trainer asked me my weight.

At the fitness centre the trainer asked me .... I weighed.

4   The exercises were easier than I expected.

The exercises weren't .... I expected.

5   You have to pay £150 a year to belong to the club.

It .... £150 a year to belong to the club.

Part 2

Question 6

Your Canadian penfriend, Brad, is coming to your country on holiday.

Write an email to Brad. In your email, you should

- offer to meet him at the airport

- suggest something you could do together one day during his holiday

- apologise for not being able to spend longer with him.

Write **35–45 words** on your answer sheet.

Part 3

Write an answer to **one** of the questions (**7** or **8**) in this part.
Write your answer in about **100 words** on your answer sheet.
Mark the question number in the box at the top of your answer sheet.

Question 7

- This is part of a letter you receive from your English friend, Linda.

> I spent all yesterday at the shopping mall and bought lots of things. Do you enjoy shopping? What sort of shops do you like best?

- Now write a letter to Linda, answering her questions.

- Write your **letter** in about 100 words on your answer sheet.

Question 8

- Your English teacher has asked you to write a story.

- This is the title for your story:

The broken window

- Write your **story** in about 100 words on your answer sheet.

Part 1

Questions 1–7

There are seven questions in this part.
For each question, there are three pictures and a short recording.
Choose the correct picture and put a tick (✓) in the box below it.

Example: Which are Sara's cousins?

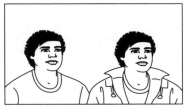

A ✓

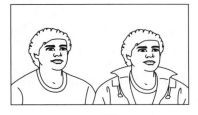

B ☐

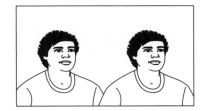

C ☐

---

1 Where does Oliver want to work?

A ☐

B ☐

C ☐

2 What will Daniel take back to the shop?

A ☐

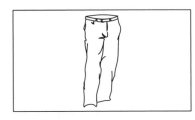

B ☐

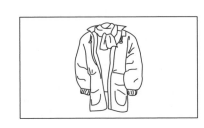

C ☐

3 What event is the woman advertising?

A ☐

B ☐

C ☐

4 Which performance did the man go to?

A ☐

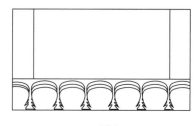

B ☐

C ☐

5 What is Jill going to talk about?

A ☐

B ☐

C ☐

6 What will the woman take to the party?

A ☐

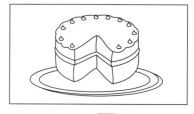

B ☐

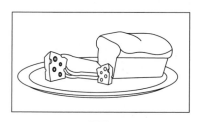

C ☐

7 What does the boy spend most time doing?

A ☐

B ☐

C ☐

Part 2

Questions 8–13

You will hear a radio interview with a woman called Holly, who runs a restaurant.
For each question, put a tick (✔) in the correct box.

8 Why did Holly start working in Palmer's Pizzas?

    A The owner asked her to help. ☐

    B She needed to earn some money. ☐

    C A friend suggested that she applied. ☐

9 What didn't Holly like about Palmer's Pizzas?

    A The work was very tiring. ☐

    B She couldn't choose the menu. ☐

    C Some of the customers were rude. ☐

10 When Holly decided to open a restaurant, it took a long time

    A to choose a suitable building. ☐

    B to raise enough money. ☐

    C to find suitable staff. ☐

11 When Holly's restaurant opened, the best thing was said by

    A a customer. ☐

    B a waiter. ☐

    C a cook. ☐

12 Holly thinks the most important thing about a restaurant is

    A keeping prices low. ☐

    B serving food of excellent quality. ☐

    C making the customers feel welcome. ☐

13 Holly is planning to

    A continue running only one restaurant. ☐

    B open several more restaurants. ☐

    C change to a different type of business. ☐

Part 3

You will hear a man talking on a local radio station about a photography competition in the town.
For each question, fill in the missing information in the numbered space.

HARTFIELD FESTIVAL

To celebrate the fact that the town is at least **(14)** ....
years old.

Photography competition

Categories:

Age 11 and under: subject is **(15)** `..'.

Age 12 to 18: subject is `Hartfield's **(16)** ....'.

Adults (19 and over): subject is **(17)** `..'.

Entry forms: download from festival website

Closing date for entries: **(18)** ....

Three prizes in each category.

Winners announced on 20th July.

Exhibition of all photos in the **(19)** .... from
August to December.

Part 4

Questions 20–25

Look at the six sentences for this part.
You will hear a conversation between a man and his daughter, Rose, who has just arrived back from a school trip by ship.
Decide if each sentence is correct or incorrect.
If it is correct, put a tick (✓) in the box under **A** for **YES**.
If it is not correct, put a tick (✓) in the box under **B** for **NO**.

		A YES	B NO
20	Rose's mother will arrive home before Rose and her father.	☐	☐
21	Rose is glad that the trip has ended.	☐	☐
22	Rose's father has been on the ship that she was on.	☐	☐
23	Rose's best friend went on the school trip.	☐	☐
24	Rose thought most of the food on the ship was very good.	☐	☐
25	Rose wants to give her mother a surprise.	☐	☐

Part 1

General conversation: saying who you are, spelling your name, giving personal information.

Take turns to be the examiner. Ask your partner questions to find out some information about each other.

Ask each other at least four of these questions:
- What's your name?
- What's your surname?
- How do you spell it?

- Where do you come from?
- Are you a student or do you work?
- What do you do/study?
- What's the weather like in the winter where you live?
- Do you think students should get a job in their free time?

Part 2

Simulated situation: giving opinions, making suggestions.

Your examiner gives you both a picture. You do a task together.

You've decided to work together during the summer holiday in temporary jobs, to improve your English. Look at page 178. There are some pictures of jobs you might be interested in. Talk about what you would like and dislike about each job. Decide what job you will both apply for.

Ask and answer questions like these:
- Which skills do we want to improve: speaking, listening, reading or writing?
- Who can we talk to while we're working?
- How can other people help us to improve our English?
- What sort of work would we both enjoy?
- What would be most useful for our English?

Part 3

You take turns to tell each other about a photograph.

Candidate A: Look at Photograph 6A on page 183.
Candidate B: Look at Photograph 6B on page 187.

Think about your photograph for a few seconds.
Describe it to your partner for about one minute.

Tell your partner about these things:
- what kind of place it is
- what the people are doing
- whether they are having a good time
- what you can guess about the music
- how the people feel about the music.

Part 4

The examiner asks you to talk to your partner. You give your opinion about something and explain what you prefer.

Tell each other about the music you like.

Use these ideas:
- Talk about what kind of music you like.
- Say whether you prefer to listen or to perform.
- Say whether you listen to music alone or with other people.
- Say whether you like to do other things while you listen to music.
- Talk about how you feel when you listen to different types of music.

Reading

Part 1

Questions 1–5

Look at the text in each question.
What does it say?
Mark the correct letter **A**, **B** or **C** on your answer sheet.

Example:

0
> Charlie,
> Please can you pick up my coat from the dry cleaner's when you collect your suit? I'll give you the money this afternoon if that's OK.
> Thanks a lot!
> Vera

What will Charlie do?

A Get paid back by Vera for the dry cleaning later today.

B Take his clothes to the dry cleaner's.

C Fetch Vera's suit from the dry cleaner's.

Answer:

1

To:	Jake
From:	Claire
Subject:	Camping trip

> Shame we both missed yesterday's meeting. Do you have contact details so we can find out what to take? I've deleted the email!

Claire is asking Jake

A how to get information about the camping trip.

B what she should take on the camping trip.

C when the camping trip is going to take place.

2

Wait until button is lit before pressing it to open the train doors.

A The light comes on automatically when the train doors open.

B You can only open the train doors when the button is lit.

C If the light is on, the train doors cannot be opened.

3

Hi Will,
Venice is beautiful – sorry you couldn't come with me. I'm leaving for Rome tomorrow. With luck, you're still there and we can travel to Naples together.
Tony

Tony hopes to meet Will in

A   Rome.

B   Naples.

C   Venice.

4

This equipment can only be moved from Lab 1 with the lab manager's permission.

A   This equipment must only be used in Lab 1.

B   Ask the manager for permission before using this equipment.

C   Permission is unnecessary if you want to use the equipment in Lab 1.

5

Tim,
Could you take this DVD to Jackie on your way to college, please? I've rung her and she knows you might come round.
Stephie

Stephie wants Tim to

A   collect a DVD from Jackie and give it to Stephie.

B   give Jackie a DVD when he is going to college.

C   phone Jackie and arrange to give her a DVD.

Part 2

Questions 6–10

The people below all want to buy a book.
On the opposite page, there are reviews of eight books.
Decide which book would be most suitable for the following people.
For questions **6–10**, mark the correct letter (**A–H**) on your answer sheet.

6

Valentina wants to become a writer herself, and she enjoys reading any books that are by famous authors and are well written. She is very keen on books that make her use her imagination.

7

Loc is studying economics and he would like to read an exciting story where money plays an important part. He likes thrillers, with plenty of action.

8

Narmin is training to become a teacher. She wants to understand what it was like to be a child in different countries in the past.

9

Shami wants a book that will help her to understand life for people who have moved to a different country. She would prefer fiction, ideally based on the writer's own experience.

10

Joe doesn't know much about science, and would like to read a book that makes it easy to understand. He's particularly interested in the history of science.

Some of This Month's New Books

A Work or Play

We think we spend our time playing or at school – until we become adults. Diego Pireno reminds us that in earlier centuries, and in some places still today, millions of children had to work. He describes the lives of typical children around the world in the last two centuries.

B The Money Book

Before money was invented, people exchanged items, or paid with anything that had a value for other people – such as shells or stones. Professor Joel Sandford explains how we started using coins and banknotes, and includes a number of surprising facts.

C Room 74

This is one of the best crime novels of the year. You won't be able to put the book down until you've reached the last page! An unlikely detective solves the mystery of a major bank robbery – but only after a series of fights, murders and amazing surprises.

D Running Wild

Jane Terry is one of our most popular authors for children and normally writes very well. I am sorry to say, though, that her latest novel is a disappointment: a character's mother suddenly becomes her aunt, people appear in places that they couldn't possibly reach, and much more.

E Why We Live As We Do

Carol Conway has written several excellent books describing daily life in the last five centuries. In her latest, however, Conway explores how science has developed in the same period, and its impact on people's lives – from electricity to plastic. People who know little or nothing about the subject will learn a lot from this book.

F Ganjeera

In *Ganjeera*, Karin Halvorsen creates strange and exciting pictures in the reader's mind, and the laws of science don't always operate. Halvorsen's skill at writing makes her one of the best-known and most popular novelists for teenagers – every word and every comma matters.

G Mexican Adventure

This is the latest in Gareth Young's long line of action novels, and as always, it's hard to guess what's going to happen next. Each of his novels is set in a different country, and the characters of *Mexican Adventure* are footballers training for an international match.

H Mountain Rose

Hussein Al-Djabri lived in Morocco until he was seven, when his father started working in Canada, and the whole family soon followed him. Al-Djabri now lives in Germany. In this novel, the hero, Abdullah, leads a life that is very similar to Al-Djabri's.

Part 3

Look at the sentences below about holidays in the Baltic Sea on board a ship.
Read the text on the opposite page to decide if each sentence is correct or incorrect.
If it is correct, mark **A** on your answer sheet.
If it is not correct, mark **B** on your answer sheet.

---

11   The company has arranged the same number of Baltic cruises as last year.

12   All the cruise ships leave from Southampton.

13   All the company's Baltic cruises follow the same route.

14   A ride on the railway near Kiristiansand is included in the cost of the cruise.

15   The company offers the chance to go to a performance in the Gothenburg opera house.

16   In Sweden, the ship visits a city which includes islands and water.

17   In Copenhagen, you will get off the ship not far from the statue of the Little Mermaid.

18   The company suggests walking around the centres of Copenhagen and Helsinki.

19   The ship stays overnight in St Petersburg.

20   The company arranges guided tours of St Petersburg.

Cruising in the Baltic Sea

The Baltic is a fascinating area, and the cities on its shores are among the most beautiful and historic in the world. Our Baltic cruises are becoming increasingly popular, and this year we are offering more cruises than ever before, so you can be sure of a starting date that suits you.

Your holiday starts at your local railway station, as our prices include travel by train from any station in the UK to Southampton, where you will join your ship. Once you are at sea you will call at a number of exciting destinations, depending on the particular cruise. For example, you might visit **Kiristiansand**, in the extreme south of Norway, a town with beaches, beautiful scenery and the **Setesdal Vintage Railway**. For an extra charge, you will have time for a three-hour ride on the train, pulled by a steam engine that is over 100 years old.

Another port where you may call is **Gothenburg**, in the south of Sweden. Its modern opera house in the harbour was designed to look like a ship, and is a very popular venue. Although our visit will be too brief to attend a performance, you will have time to see the building and the city. Stockholm is another place you'll enjoy visiting. Much of Sweden's capital is on islands, and a third of the city consists of water.

Copenhagen, the capital of Denmark, is famous for its statue of the **Little Mermaid**, a character in a children's story by the Danish writer Hans Christian Andersen. This is only a short distance from where you leave the ship. But there is plenty more to see in the city. Like Copenhagen, **Helsinki**, the Finnish capital, is small enough to explore the historical centre on foot, and they're

both ideal cities for shopping – the Scandinavian countries are famous for their design!

For many of our passengers, the best part of a cruise is a visit to **St Petersburg**. The city dates from 1703 and for two hundred years it was the Russian capital. All our cruises include the city, and you will have two full days in port here, giving you plenty of time to admire the beautiful palaces, churches and other buildings. If you'd like a guided tour, there are plenty available – on foot, by car or by boat along the city's rivers and canals – although unfortunately we no longer organise tours ourselves.

Among the many other cities that you can visit on our Baltic cruises are **Tallinn, Riga and Oslo**.

For more details visit our website.

• •

Read the text and questions below.
For each question, mark the correct letter **A**, **B**, **C** or **D** on your answer sheet.

Life as a Hotel Manager

by Kirsty Jenkins

Some hotels have hundreds of rooms, some have just a few. You might think small hotels are friendlier, but making guests feel welcome isn't a question of size but of attitude. Guests can be made to feel at home in a 900-room hotel with a swimming pool and half a dozen restaurants, and unwelcome in a hotel with a few bedrooms and just a small breakfast room. It all depends on the employees, from receptionists to cleaners to managers.

Many people start working in hotels to meet people, or to provide a good service. My own reason was much less interesting: I left university, my parents had moved abroad, and I had to find a job with accommodation. I went into the first hotel I saw, and asked if they had any jobs. Luckily, a receptionist had just left, and I was offered the job – together with a room in the staff part of the hotel.

I loved the work and soon decided to aim for hotel management. Now, ten years later, I run a 20-room, independent hotel that was recently named 'Small Hotel of the Year' by a national newspaper. Of course it's great when guests tell you they've really enjoyed their stay or their meal and want to return. And our restaurant menu attracts both guests and local people. Hotel staff often don't stay in their jobs long because they're unhappy with the manager. Before I started at this hotel, almost all its employees left within a year. My main achievement so far is that now only a third do. My aim is to reduce that figure even more.

21 What is Kirsty Jenkins trying to do in the text?

A Describe her experience of working in hotels.

B Encourage people to become hotel managers.

C Explain the difficulties of working in a hotel.

D Compare hotels now with those of the past.

22 What does Kirsty consider most important for making guests enjoy their stay?

    A The facilities.

    B The number of rooms.

    C The number of staff.

    D The way that staff behave.

23 Kirsty started working in hotels because

    A she wanted to meet a large number of people.

    B she was contacted by a hotel that needed staff.

    C she was looking for somewhere to live.

    D she wanted to be able to provide a good service.

24 In her present job, Kirsty is particularly proud that

    A many guests return to the hotel.

    B staff stay in their jobs longer than before.

    C the hotel has won a competition.

    D she has opened a successful hotel restaurant.

25 Which of these is an advertisement for the hotel that Kirsty manages?

A
> Small hotel with friendly staff. Breakfast is provided, and we are near several restaurants that are open for dinner.

B
> Hotel with just a few rooms and a restaurant open to the public. Our staff enjoy working here and they make sure you feel welcome.

C
> Large modern hotel with plenty of facilities, including swimming pool and a choice of restaurants.

D
> We are part of a chain of small hotels offering the very best in comfort. Our restaurant has won prizes for its food and service.

Part 5

Questions 26–35

Read the text below and choose the correct word for each space.
For each question, mark the correct letter **A**, **B**, **C** or **D** on your answer sheet.

Example:

0	**A**	effect	**B**	point	**C**	idea	**D** aspect

Answer:

0	A	B	C	D
	▬ (marked)			

The Skies Above

The weather has a big **(0)** .... on our lives. Consider the difference **(26)** .... waking up on a bright, sunny morning and waking up on a dark, wet and cold morning. Don't you feel positive in the first case and maybe sad in the second? We use weather words to **(27)** .... about the way we feel. For example, if somebody **(28)** .... angry, their face 'clouds over'.

We do different things **(29)** .... to what the weather's like. How **(30)** .... are you on walking in the park on a rainy day? We think about the weather before we choose what clothes to **(31)** .... on each morning.

Now consider your house: is it designed to **(32)** .... the heat out, or is it designed to **(33)** .... you from being too cold? The weather decides **(34)** .... your house is designed.

Finally, people in business often need to pay attention **(35)** .... changes in the weather. A company that makes ice cream or umbrellas must be ready with enough to sell on hot days or wet days.

26	**A** with	**B** between	**C** of	**D** among
27	**A** inform	**B** tell	**C** describe	**D** talk
28	**A** becomes	**B** goes	**C** makes	**D** runs
29	**A** allowing	**B** depending	**C** following	**D** according
30	**A** keen	**B** enjoyable	**C** happy	**D** popular
31	**A** take	**B** get	**C** put	**D** set
32	**A** continue	**B** keep	**C** contain	**D** stay
33	**A** miss	**B** avoid	**C** prevent	**D** turn
34	**A** where	**B** how	**C** that	**D** so
35	**A** on	**B** by	**C** to	**D** in

Writing

Part 1

Questions 1–5

Here are some sentences about someone who is planning to visit the river Amazon.
For each question, complete the second sentence so that it means the same as the first.
Use no more than three words.
Write only the missing words on your answer sheet.
You may use this page for any rough work.

Example:

0   The Amazon is around 6,500 kilometres long.

The .... of the Amazon is around 6,500 kilometres.

Answer: | **0** | length |

---

1   It's always been a dream of mine to see the Amazon.

It's always been one of .... to see the Amazon.

2   I want to walk in the rain forest beside the river.

I want to go .... a walk in the rain forest beside the river.

3   I can't go to the Amazon if I don't save a lot of money.

I can't go to the Amazon unless .... a lot of money.

4   I'm going to the Amazon next year for two weeks.

When I .... to the Amazon next year, I'll stay for two weeks.

5   I had to book early because so many people want to go.

I had to book early because .... a lot of people want to go.

Part 2

Question 6

Your American friend, Joanna, is going to stay with your family next weekend.

Write an email to Joanna. In your email, you should

- suggest something to do during her visit

- ask her about any food that she doesn't like

- offer to meet her at the station.

Write **35–45 words** on your answer sheet.

Part 3

Write an answer to **one** of the questions (**7** or **8**) in this part.
Write your answer in about **100 words** on your answer sheet.
Mark the question number in the box at the top of your answer sheet.

Question 7

- This is part of a letter you receive from your Irish friend, Duncan.

> I'm going to my cousin's wedding tomorrow. I'm really looking forward to it. What about weddings in your country? Do many people go? What do you eat?

- Now write a letter to Duncan, answering his questions.

- Write your **letter** in about 100 words on your answer sheet.

Question 8

- Your English teacher has asked you to write a story.

- Your story must begin with this sentence:

  The camera my brother gave me was the best present I received on my birthday.

- Write your **story** in about 100 words on your answer sheet.

Part 1

Questions 1–7

There are seven questions in this part.
For each question, there are three pictures and a short recording.
Choose the correct picture and put a tick (✓) in the box below it.

Example: Which are Sara's cousins?

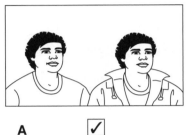

A ✓

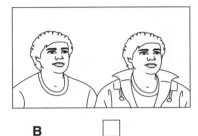

B ☐

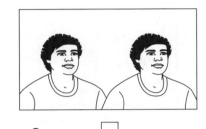

C ☐

---

1 How does the man go home from work?

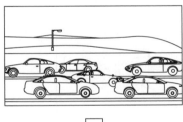

A ☐

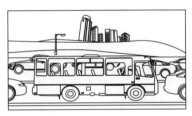

B ☐

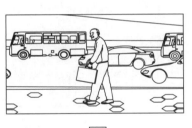

C ☐

2 Who did Sophie go shopping with?

A ☐

B ☐

C ☐

3 Who can callers see at the health centre today?

A ☐

B ☐

C ☐

4   Which painting do they decide to buy?

   **A** ☐

   **B** ☐

   **C** ☐

5   Where is the man's computer now?

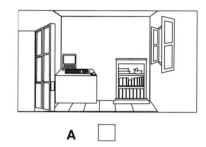   **A** ☐

   **B** ☐

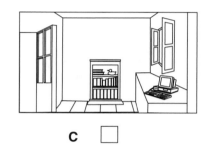   **C** ☐

6   Which building will Carl take photographs of?

   **A** ☐

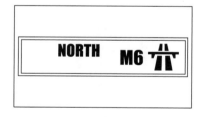   **B** ☐

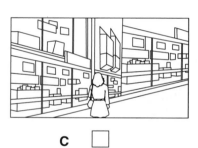   **C** ☐

7   Which road is closed at the moment?

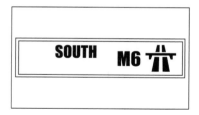   **A** ☐

   **B** ☐

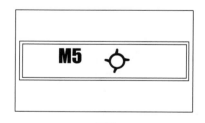   **C** ☐

Part 2

Questions 8–13

You will hear a man talking on a local radio station about the city's Spring Festival.
For each question, put a tick (✓) in the correct box.

8   What are we told about River Day?

    A   The public have requested it. ☐

    B   People can join in some activities. ☐

    C   Some of the events are new. ☐

9   On River Day, people will see

    A   sailing and motor boats. ☐

    B   a boat race. ☐

    C   copies of old boats. ☐

10   The five-mile Fun Run

    A   is limited to adults. ☐

    B   is happening for the first time. ☐

    C   is taking place in the morning. ☐

11   For the sound and light show, people should start at

    A   the harbour. ☐

    B   the city hall. ☐

    C   the university. ☐

12   The street market will include

    A   food from other countries. ☐

    B   a variety of performers. ☐

    C   activities for children. ☐

13   How is the Spring Festival different from previous festivals?

    A   The cost of organising it is higher. ☐

    B   It has taken longer to organise. ☐

    C   More people helped to organise it. ☐

Part 3

Questions 14–19

You will hear a woman talking to a group of young people about a youth club that she helps to organise. For each question, fill in the missing information in the numbered space.

Spotlight Youth Club

Full-time youth worker: Caroline.

More than 200 members.

In two sections, open to people aged from 8 to **(14)** ....

Open Monday – Friday evenings, and all day during weekends and school holidays.

Sports activities: **(15)** .... team has just won a competition.

Arts activity: most popular is **(16)** ....

Outdoor activities: next one is **(17)** .... in the Lake District.

Dates: last weekend in **(18)** ....

Cost: £65 including accommodation, food and transport by **(19)** ....

Part 4

Questions 20–25

Look at the six sentences for this part.
You will hear a conversation between a boy, Robbie, and a girl, Collette, about learning to swim.
Decide if each sentence is correct or incorrect.
If it is correct, put a tick (✓) in the box under **A** for **YES**.
If it is not correct, put a tick (✓) in the box under **B** for **NO**.

		A YES	B NO
20	Collette learned to swim several years ago.	☐	☐
21	Robbie was taught to swim by his cousin.	☐	☐
22	Robbie prefers swimming in the sea to swimming in a swimming pool.	☐	☐
23	Collette would like to swim from England to France.	☐	☐
24	Robbie goes swimming at least once a week.	☐	☐
25	Collette and Robbie arrange to have a swimming race.	☐	☐

TEST 7

Part 1

General conversation: saying who you are, spelling your name, giving personal information.

Take turns to be the examiner. Ask your partner questions to find out some information about each other.

Ask each other at least four of these questions:
• What's your name?
• What's your surname?

• How do you spell it?
• Where do you come from?
• Are you a student or do you work?
• What do you do/study?
• What do you like about the place where you live?
• What do you think you will do next weekend?

Part 2

Simulated situation: giving opinions, saying what you think other people would like.

Your examiner gives you both a picture. You do a task together.

It will soon be your neighbours' 25th wedding anniversary, and you have decided to give them a present. Look at page 179. There are some ideas of presents you could give them. Decide together what you will give them. You can only give them one thing.

Ask and answer questions like these:
• What sort of things do they like?
• Would they prefer something to keep, or something to remember?
• Would that be too expensive?
• Are we sure they would like that?
• Have we got time to buy it?

Part 3

Responding to photographs: describing where people are and what they are doing.

You take turns to tell each other about a photograph.

Candidate A: Look at Photograph 7A on page 184.
Candidate B: Look at Photograph 7B on page 188.

Think about your photograph for a few seconds.
Describe it to your partner for about one minute.

Tell your partner about these things:
* what kind of place it is
* what the relationship is between the people
* what the people are eating
* what they are wearing
* whether they are enjoying themselves.

Part 4

General conversation about the photographs: talking about food, eating and preferences.

The examiner asks you to talk to your partner.
You give your opinion about something and
explain what you prefer.

Tell each other about food that you like.

Use these ideas:
* Talk about what kinds of food you like or don't like eating.
* Say whether you like to try food you haven't eaten before.
* Talk about where you prefer to eat, and why.
* Say whether you like (or would like) to cook.
* Say whether you like to do other things while you're eating.

Reading

Part 1

Questions 1–5

Look at the text in each question.
What does it say?
Mark the correct letter **A**, **B** or **C** on your answer sheet.

Example:

0

> Charlie,
> Please can you pick up my coat from the dry cleaner's when you collect your suit? I'll give you the money this afternoon if that's OK. Thanks a lot!
> Vera

What will Charlie do?

A Get paid back by Vera for the dry cleaning later today.

B Take his clothes to the dry cleaner's.

C Fetch Vera's suit from the dry cleaner's.

Answer:

0	A	B	C
	▰	▱	▱

1

> Mai,
> Could you look up the train timetable and let me know the earliest you can manage tomorrow? We can meet at the station 20 minutes before it leaves.
> Juanita

Mai should

A contact Juanita after deciding what train they should catch tomorrow.

B find out the time of the earliest train that runs tomorrow.

C meet Juanita at the station so they can choose which train to catch.

2

No items of value are left in this shop outside opening hours.

A No valuable objects are kept in this shop at any time.

B Valuable objects are removed from the shop when it is closed.

C If you leave any valuable objects in the shop, they will be kept safely.

3

To:	Majeda
From:	Sandy
Subject:	Mushroom curry

Could you email your mushroom curry recipe, please? I'd like to make it for my party on Saturday. Sorry you'll miss it.

A Sandy is asking Majeda to help him cook some food on Saturday.

B Sandy wants to find out how to cook a mushroom curry.

C Sandy hopes that Majeda will be able to come to his party.

4

Touch screen to check in. Then wait for doctor to call your name.

A Use this screen to let the doctor know that you have arrived.

B Your name will appear on the screen when the doctor is ready for you.

C Check that your appointment is shown in the list on the screen.

5

Roland,
Dad's train's due 6 p.m. but I can't get there. Could you meet him and take him to your place? I'll get there as soon as I can.
Karen

Karen hopes to see Dad

A at her home.

B at the train station.

C at Roland's home.

Part 2

Questions 6–10

The people below all want to do a course in their free time.
On the opposite page, there is information about eight courses in a college brochure.
Decide which course would be most suitable for the following people.
For questions **6–10**, mark the correct letter (**A–H**) on your answer sheet.

6

Aftab enjoys reading novels, plays and poetry in Arabic, French and English. He would like a course that uses his skills, and where he can study at home for a different number of hours each week.

7

Yuan spends all week sitting at a computer, and she wants to do something physical and active on Saturdays. She would prefer an activity where she does something with other people.

8

Andries has never done anything creative, and he would like to learn to paint. However, he works different hours each week, so he doesn't want a course at a fixed time.

9

Tina doesn't have a job. She likes making clothes for friends, cutting their hair and experimenting with make-up. She wants a course that will help her get a job where she can use these interests.

10

Mischa works at a sports centre but can take one day off each week to study. He would like to train for a new job where he can fix machines of some sort.

Calliston College: leisure courses

A **Save money by learning how to repair your own car engine** – or even qualify as a car mechanic. This is a course where you have plenty to do, and very little to read. You'll learn how engines are made, and have a lot of practice at repairing them. 9 a.m. until 4 p.m. every Tuesday.

B Join our **'Introduction to World Literature'** course! There's a weekly Wednesday evening class, and instead of homework, we suggest books you can read in your own time – in the original language or in translation. So you decide how much time you spend reading each week

C Are you afraid to **use a computer?** That can easily be changed! Join our computer class for beginners and you'll soon discover that it's much easier than you thought. Classes are held every day from Monday to Saturday, and you can come whichever day you like – and a different day each week, if you want to!

D **Football** for men and women! Even if you've never played before, come along on Monday evenings and have some fun. Ideal if you spend most of the day sitting down. We have several teams and there's sure to be one at the right level for you.

E Whether you're a beginner or advanced, you can **study art** at the college. You'll learn to draw and to use oils. Instead of regular classes, one of our tutors will be available every day and evening, so you can come in when it's convenient for you.

F If you can spend the whole of every Thursday at the college, why not consider our **fashion and beauty course?** It prepares you for a range of careers, including hairdressing, fashion design and the theatre. Most employers will give you time off to attend.

G Have you ever thought about **reading aloud?** We run classes where you'll make new friends, and learn to read well. Many of our students get work with a company that records both children's and adults' books.

H If you like being part of a team, and want to do some **exercise to keep fit**, our swimming team is the perfect choice! It meets every Saturday morning and prepares for both competitions and displays. You don't have to be a good swimmer – we'll teach you if necessary.

Part 3

Look at the sentences below about the city of Cork in the Republic of Ireland.
Read the text on the opposite page to decide if each sentence is correct or incorrect.
If it is correct, mark **A** on your answer sheet.
If it is not correct, mark **B** on your answer sheet.

---

11   Cork has the biggest population of any city in the Republic of Ireland, except Dublin.

12   Cork has more railway lines now than it did in the nineteenth century.

13   The centre of Cork is surrounded by water.

14   Cork is situated on the sea coast.

15   Cork Historic Walking Tours arranges several different tours of the city each day.

16   The walks arranged by Cork Historic Walking Tours take place every day throughout the year.

17   You can have unlimited travel on a company's buses for a day with one ticket.

18   The prison was built on the site of an old castle.

19   A radio station was based inside the prison building in the 1920s.

20   In the past, food was bought in Cork and taken to shops in England.

The City of Cork, Republic of Ireland

With a **population of** around 120,000, Cork is the second-largest city in the Republic of Ireland, after the capital, Dublin. Cork has always been an important port and, during the nineteenth century, it also became the centre of a major rail network covering the southwest of Ireland. Many of these lines have since closed, however.

The city is **built on the river Lee**, which rises in the mountains west of Cork. For a short distance, it divides into two main channels, creating the island on which the city centre is situated. The two parts of the river then join, and the Lee flows on to the port. Ships sail down the river the few miles that separate Cork from the open sea.

The best way to **explore Cork** is on foot. Cork Historic Walking Tours offers tours of the city, which will show you how it has developed over the centuries. There are a number of tours each day, every one exploring a different period in the city's history. The tours are led by qualified guides, and take place on Mondays to Fridays, from the beginning of April until the end of September.

Or you might prefer to see the city from the comfort of an **open-top bus**, operated by a local bus company. Just buy a day ticket and you'll be free to get off one bus and get on another as many times as you like during the day.

There is plenty to see in Cork, from **historic buildings** to **art galleries**, and one of the most interesting attractions is the old prison, the **Cork City Gaol**. With its high walls to prevent prisoners from escaping, this magnificent building was built to look like a castle. Visit the prison to find out what life was like for the people who were held here between 1824 and 1923. Tours of the prison are available in up to 13 languages.

In the 1920s **a radio station** opened in part of the former prison, and this building is now the home of the **Radio Museum Experience**. The museum has recreated the studio that was first used here in 1927. The exhibition also shows how radio has influenced our lives since then.

And Cork is a perfect city for **shopping!** For example, the English Market has stalls selling food from all over the world. It is over 200 years old, and the name comes from the fact that in its early days, English businesses bought food here to resell in shops in England. Cork also has plenty of stores, large and small, from major department stores to smart independent shops.

• • • • • • • • • • • • • •

Part 4

Read the text and questions below.
For each question, mark the correct letter **A**, **B**, **C** or **D** on your answer sheet.

Australia's Harmony Day

There are 22 million Australians. Some families have lived in the country for thousands of years, others for a century or two. Nearly half the population were either born abroad themselves, or have at least one parent who was. There are people from over 200 cultural backgrounds. One in six Australians speak a language other than English at home — a total of over 300 languages. Harmony Day is an annual celebration of this wide range of cultures.

Since the first Harmony Day, in 1999, thousands of schools, clubs and other organisations have arranged events, and the number is growing. Sport, food, dance — all are ways of bringing together people from different cultures. The celebrations have even reached across the ocean, with a video link between a school class in Australia and one in Italy.

Last year, some teenagers in Sydney made a DVD about people who had moved there from other countries. They filmed five people chatting about why they had moved, and comparing life in Australia and in the countries where they were born. The DVD was shown at a party attended by over 200 people from various cultures.

In another example, a Japanese club held a fashion show, where men, women and children dressed in traditional clothes from their own cultures and talked about them. Takeshi, one of the organisers, thought it was very exciting. He was delighted that many of the people there were happy to live in Australia and to have a cultural background from another country.

If you're thinking of organising a Harmony Day event, there is a government department which can advise you. Unfortunately, though, they can't help you meet the cost.

21 What is the writer's main purpose in writing the text?

A To request suggestions for improving Harmony Day.

B To encourage organisations to arrange an event.

C To introduce a programme of events.

D To review the last Harmony Day.

22 One year, a group of Italian children

    A   Visited Australia to take part in the celebrations.

    B   Welcomed some Australian children to their homes.

    C   Celebrated Harmony Day in their own school.

    D   Contacted some Australian children to show their support.

23 What did the DVD made by teenagers in Sydney show?

    A   One person talking about the benefits of living in Australia.

    B   A discussion about life in Australia and in other countries.

    C   One person explaining why they had moved to Australia.

    D   Several people saying what they missed in Australia.

24 What does Takeshi say about the fashion show?

    A   He was surprised there were people from so many cultures.

    B   He changed his ideas about other cultures.

    C   He was pleased the Japanese club was the venue.

    D   He met many people who were proud of their culture.

25 Which of these is part of a report by the Australian government?

A

Harmony Day is an experiment. If it is successful, we'll continue to provide money for it.

B

More and more groups organise events for Harmony Day, helping people to understand each other's cultures.

C

Although Harmony Day takes place in Australia, we insist that organisers make contact with groups in other countries.

D

Harmony Day shows that without the English language, it would be very difficult for Australians from different cultures to communicate with each other.

Part 5

Read the text below and choose the correct word for each space.
For each question, mark the correct letter **A**, **B**, **C** or **D** on your answer sheet.

Example:

0   **A**   is   **B**   becomes   **C**   has   **D**   gets

Answer: | 0 | A ▬ B ☐ C ☐ D ☐ |

Bill Mackston

Bill's Mackston's life today **(0)** .... a very different one
from **(26)** .... it used to be. For as **(27)** .... as
anybody could remember, Bill wanted to make money. Even as
a young boy at school, he started up small businesses: using
tools he **(28)** .... from his father, he **(29)** .... bikes
that didn't work properly, **(30)** .... half the price of the
bike shop nearby.

After he left school, he **(31)** .... a series of companies, each one more successful
than **(32)** .... last. He **(33)** .... tens of thousands of people in several
countries. He had seven houses, a helicopter, a plane, two boats, twenty cars …

But Bill was actually very lonely, and never knew **(34)** .... his many friends liked
him or his money more. So one day he gave everything **(35)** .... He just stopped.
Now he lives on a very small farm, where he grows vegetables, and sits, and thinks …

26   **A** what   **B** when   **C** who   **D** which

27   **A** old   **B** far   **C** much   **D** long

28   **A** borrowed   **B** lent   **C** gave   **D** presented

29   **A** fixed   **B** turned   **C** changed   **D** stuck

30   **A** telling   **B** charging   **C** making   **D** numbering

31   **A** went   **B** moved   **C** ran   **D** continued

32   **A** its   **B** the   **C** a   **D** this

33   **A** practised   **B** included   **C** applied   **D** employed

34   **A** that   **B** how   **C** if   **D** it

35   **A** over   **B** off   **C** up   **D** out

Writing

Part 1

Questions 1–5

Here are some sentences about a visit to the cinema.
For each question, complete the second sentence so that it means the same as the first.
Use no more than three words.
Write only the missing words on your answer sheet.
You may use this page for any rough work.

Example:

0   I think it's always fun to go to the cinema.

   I think that ………… **to the cinema is always fun.**

Answer: | **0** | *going* |

---

1   I usually go to the cinema two or more times a month.

   I usually go to the cinema ………… **twice a month.**

2   I prefer films about ordinary people to action films.

   I'd rather see films about ordinary people ………… **action films.**

3   Sometimes there are such a lot of good films that I can't see them all.

   Sometimes there are ………… **many good films for me to see them all.**

4   Not all films attract a large audience.

   Not every ………… **a large audience.**

5   I don't enjoy horror films as much as other films.

   I think horror films are ………… **enjoyable than others.**

Part 2

Question 6

Your Welsh friend, Steve, is going to his grandfather's birthday party soon.

Write an email to Steve. In your email you should

- suggest a birthday present

- explain why it would be a good present

- offer to help him buy the present.

Write **35–45 words** on your answer sheet.

Part 3

Write an answer to **one** of the questions (**7** or **8**) in this part.
Write your answer in about **100 words** on your answer sheet.
Mark the question number in the box at the top of your answer sheet.

Question 7

- This is part of a letter you receive from your Australian penfriend, Amanda.

> I played a lot of tennis yesterday. It was great! Do you play or watch any sport? What's your favourite sport? Why do you like it?

- Now write a letter to Amanda, answering her questions.

- Write your **letter** in about 100 words on your answer sheet.

Question 8

- Your English teacher has asked you to write a story.

- Your story must begin with this sentence:

  ### When Sharon arrived, everyone was really surprised to see her.

- Write your **story** in about 100 words on your answer sheet.

Part 1

Questions 1–7

There are seven questions in this part.
For each question, there are three pictures and a short recording.
Choose the correct picture and put a tick (✓) in the box below it.

Example: Which are Sara's cousins?

A ✓

B ☐

C ☐

---

1 When will the youth orchestra's concert take place?

A ☐

B ☐

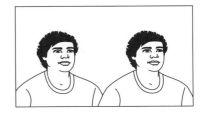

C ☐

2 Where did the woman spend her holiday?

A ☐

B ☐

C ☐

3 Where does the man live?

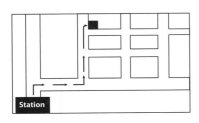

A ☐

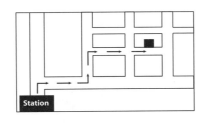

B ☐

C ☐

4   What has the man just found?

A ☐   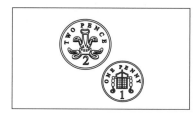   B ☐      C ☐

5   What is particularly cheap at the moment?

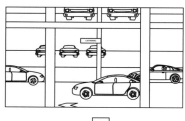   A ☐   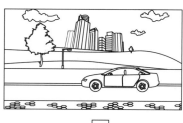   B ☐   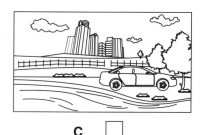   C ☐

6   Where has the woman parked her car?

   A ☐      B ☐      C ☐

7   Where are they going to eat?

A ☐   B ☐   C ☐

Part 2

Questions 8–13

You will hear an actor called Gwen talking to a group of drama students.
For each question, put a tick (✓) in the correct box.

---

8 Why did Gwen want to become a professional actor?

    A She enjoyed being the centre of attention. ☐

    B She wanted to meet famous actors. ☐

    C She liked the atmosphere in the theatre. ☐

9 Gwen was first paid as an actor

    A when she was a child. ☐

    B when she was at drama college. ☐

    C when she joined a theatre company. ☐

10 Gwen is most interested in roles that are

    A very different from her. ☐

    B similar to people she knows. ☐

    C the sort of person she would like to be. ☐

11 Gwen advises the students to spend their free time

    A getting to know other people. ☐

    B reading plays. ☐

    C going to the theatre. ☐

12 Gwen wants the students to perform a play by

    A a friend of hers. ☐

    B a famous writer of plays. ☐

    C an unknown writer. ☐

13 Gwen offers to help the student production by

    A acting in the play. ☐

    B giving advice about the play. ☐

    C encouraging people to attend the play. ☐

Part 3

Questions 14–19

You will hear a man talking about a shopping trip that he has organised for some college students. For each question, fill in the missing information in the numbered space.

Shopping trip to Burlington next Wednesday morning

Meeting place: at the (14) .... of the college.

Meeting time: (15) ....

One group will go with Zac to a (16) .... store.

The other group will go with Laura to the biggest (17) .... store in the city, on Westchester Road.

Bring packed lunch to eat at picnic tables on the (18) ....

Afternoon: free time

Departure time 4.00 p.m. from bus station on (19) ....

Part 4

Questions 20–25

Look at the six sentences for this part.
You will hear a conversation between a man, Jack, and his neighbour, Hayley, about Capworth, the town where they live.
Decide if each sentence is correct or incorrect.
If it is correct, put a tick (✓) in the box under **A** for **YES**.
If it is not correct, put a tick (✓) in the box under **B** for **NO**.

		A YES	B NO
20	Jack has lived in Capworth all his life.	☐	☐
21	Jack thinks people in Capworth are friendlier than they used to be.	☐	☐
22	Jack believes the new school is in the wrong location.	☐	☐
23	Hayley likes the design of the new school.	☐	☐
24	Hayley supports the idea of building a new leisure centre.	☐	☐
25	Jack may help to run the new leisure centre.	☐	☐

Part 1

General conversation: saying who you are, spelling your name, giving personal information.

Take turns to be the examiner. Ask your partner questions to find out some information about each other.

Ask each other at least four of these questions:
- What's your name?
- What's your surname?

- How do you spell it?
- Where do you come from?
- Are you a student or do you work?
- What do you do/study?
- Why are you studying English?
- What different things do you do in the summer and winter?

Part 2

Simulated situation: giving opinions, saying what you think other people would like.

Your examiner gives you both a picture. You do a task together.

Some friends with a young child want to go away on holiday for two weeks. Talk together about where they should go. Look at page 180. Decide together where they should go.

Ask and answer questions like these:
- What sort of things do the parents like doing?
- How can they keep their child entertained?
- What facilities do they need for the child?
- Is there anyone who can look after the child while the parents go out?
- Do they want to cook for themselves?

Part 3

Responding to photographs: describing a job and a workplace.

You take turns to tell each other about a photograph.

Candidate A: Look at Photograph 8A on page 184.
Candidate B: Look at Photograph 8B on page 188.

Think about your photograph for a few seconds.
Describe it to your partner for about one minute.

Tell your partner about these things:
• what kind of place it is
• what you can see there
• what the people are doing
• how the people feel about their jobs
• whether their work is always like this.

Part 4

General conversation about the photographs: talking about likes, dislikes and jobs.

The examiner asks you to talk to your partner.
You give your opinion about something and
explain what you prefer.

Tell each other about jobs you might like.

Use these ideas:
• Say whether you have a job or would like to
  have one.
• Say how you feel (or may feel in the future) about
  the job, and why.
• Talk about what types of job you would enjoy.
• Say what types of job you wouldn't enjoy.
• Talk about whether the people you work with are
  important to you.

Resources

Speaking File

This Speaking File contains useful language for you to use in the four parts of the Speaking Test, as well as exercises designed to help you prepare for the Test.

Speaking Part 1: General conversation

The examiner will ask you questions. Be prepared to give suitable answers about you and your life.

Introducing yourself

My name's/I'm Andre Simonoviescz.
My friends call me Andy.

Giving information about yourself

Practise saying sentences like these about yourself:

I come from a (small/large) family.
I'm an only child.
I've got (an older brother) and (two younger sisters).
I live with (my parents).
I share a flat with (some other students).
My home's in (the city centre/a suburb/a small village).
I live and work in (London).
I'm studying (chemical engineering).
I'm training to be a (train driver).
I'm a (teacher).
I work in (publishing).
I get up (quite early) every morning.
I go out with (my friends most evenings).
I don't have a lot of spare time, but when I can, I like to (go to the cinema).
In my spare time, I (do a lot of sport).
My hobby is (gardening).

Exercise 1

Look at these things students said in their exam.
Choose the missing words from the box to fill the gaps.
Use each word only once.

when	do	at	got	about	have	near	takes

1 I've .... two older sisters.
2 I'm training to be an architect, but it .... a long time.
3 I'm studying modern languages .... university.

4 I .... to get up very early in the morning because it's a long way to my school.
5 Our flat's in the old part of the city, ... the main square.
6 I hope to work in marketing in the future, and I think I'll need English to .... that.
7 Although I don't have very much spare time, I go cycling .... I can.
8 I go to college by bus every day and it takes .... half an hour.

Speaking Part 2: Discussing a situation

You will have to discuss a situation, based on pictures, with your partner. Be ready to share ideas and opinions.

Asking for and making suggestions

Which (activity) do you think would be best?
What about (going swimming in the river)?
We could try (climbing trees).
I think (mountain biking) would be a good idea.
What do you think we should do?
Let's choose (the horse-riding).
Why don't we choose (the diving)?

Giving and explaining opinions

I think (a book) is best because it's (interesting).
In my opinion, (a plant) is a good idea. It (will last a long time and look pretty).
I think we should (buy her a watch) because (she hasn't got one and she's always late).

Asking for opinions

What about you?
What do you think?
Do you think (swimming) would be a good idea?
Do you agree?

Agreeing

I really agree with you.
OK, let's choose that one.
That's a good idea.
That sounds right.
That's true/right.
That's a good point.
Of course.
Definitely!
That's probably right/true.
I suppose/guess so.

Disagreeing

Maybe that's not such a great idea.
I don't know if that's the best idea.
I don't think so.
Definitely not!
I can't agree with that.
Perhaps you're right, but …
In my opinion, that isn't true.
I see what you mean, but I think …

Accepting that you have different opinions

Let's agree to disagree.
I don't suppose we'll ever agree about this.

Exercise 2

These sentences taken from a student's comments in their speaking exam are jumbled up. Put the words into the correct order.

1   do of you these which useful would be one think most?

   ....

2   agree is I one that best this the

   ....

3   we choose don't one why that?

   ....

4   best the that's perhaps way not

   ....

5   about I never we'll agree this guess

   ....

6   I but mean you what prefer see I the one first

   ....

Speaking Part 3: Describing a photo

You will talk about a photograph. You need to be able to describe different aspects of the photograph.

Describing the position of things in a photograph

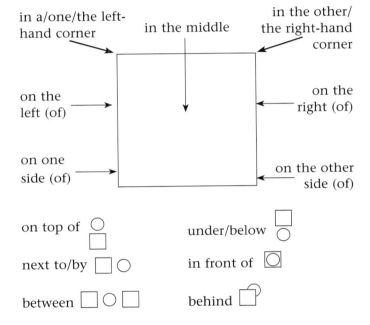

In the background, there are some trees.
In the foreground, I can see two people standing.

There's a tall man holding a horse.
I can see a car driving along a big road.
On the left of the photo, there's a café with seats outside.
The table is near the window.
It's quite dark inside the room.

Saying where the people are

They're standing indoors/outdoors/by a river, etc.
They're sitting on a train/bus, etc.
They're at the beach/in a swimming pool/at a party/in a big room, etc.
They seem to be in a hotel/cinema/forest, etc.

Describing people

She's (quite/rather) short/tall/thin/fat, etc.
He's got dark/fair skin/hair, etc.
She's got short/long/straight hair, etc.
He's wearing jeans and a strange hat, etc.

Describing places

The (square) looks rather crowded.
It seems to be a very (old) (bridge).
There aren't very many (people) in the (street).
The (countryside) looks very (beautiful).
It's very (sunny) at (the beach).

Making guesses

I think they look rather sad/quite happy, etc.
They seem a bit bored/tired to me, etc.
It looks as if they're having fun/problems, etc.
Something must be (funny) because (they're laughing).
I'm not sure, but I think it might be (in China),
because of (the buildings).
I don't know what this is, but I guess it's a ...
I suppose they could be (friends or sisters).
He's probably a (famous person), because
(everyone's looking at him).
Maybe they're (lost).
Perhaps they (don't know which way to go).

Exercise 3

Look at these descriptions of people in photos. For each gap, choose the correct word.

1   The man's hair *looks/is* .... very short.
2   I think she's probably only about 15 *years/years old* ....
3   He might be rich – he's wearing very smart *clothes/dress* ....
4   Maybe they're on holiday, because they *seem/suppose* .... very relaxed.
5   She's winning the race, because the other runners are a long way *before/behind* .... her.
6   They could *come/take* .... from the same family.
7   I think he's worried *because/when* .... he's going to miss his flight.
8   When I *watch/see* .... the cake, it makes me think it's someone's birthday.

Speaking Part 4: Discussion

You will discuss a topic with your partner. Be prepared to exchange and compare opinions and experiences.

Giving and responding to opinions

In my opinion, it's ...
I think/believe that ... because ...
Do you agree?
What do you think?
Are you sure?
How about you?

Expressing and asking about likes and dislikes

Do you like (playing tennis)?
What do you (like/enjoy)?
I enjoy (watching TV programmes that make me laugh).
I'm not very keen on (noisy restaurants).
I'm most interested in (music from Africa).
My favourite kind of (food is seafood/music is hip hop), etc.
I'm less keen on (riding my bike in the city).
I like/don't like (watching sport) because ...
I'd rather live in (the city centre) than (a small town).
I like the (beach), but I prefer (the mountains).
I suppose if I could choose, I would (live in a big house in the forest).

Exercise 4

Look at this discussion between two candidates in the exam. Choose the correct words and phrases from the box to fill the gaps.

> not very   opinion   about you   Really
> don't suppose   because   Actually
> I think   I'd rather   prefer
> on them   about this

Candidate A: Well, I **(1)** .... playing sport to watching sport on TV because I like to try to keep fit. It feels strange to sit on a sofa doing nothing but watching people running around. How **(2)** .... ?

Candidate B: It's an interesting question. To be honest, I'm **(3)** .... keen on playing sport. In fact, **(4)** .... go and watch a movie, or go to a restaurant with my friends than watch sport, or play sport.

Candidate A: **(5)** .... ? You don't like sport at all?

Candidate B: **(6)** .... , I enjoy very big sporting events. For example, my favourite is the world cup football. I find it exciting **(7)** .... the players are the best in the world.

Candidate A: In my **(8)** .... it's more interesting to watch games between smaller clubs.

Candidate B: I'm not so keen **(9)** ....

Candidate A: The best thing is to actually play the sport yourself, **(10)** ....

Candidate B: I **(11)** .... we'll ever agree **(12)** ....

Speaking: All parts

When you don't understand

Could you repeat that, please?
Could you say that again, please?
Please you could explain what we have to do?
I don't understand what you want me to do.

When you don't know the name of something

I don't know what this is called in English.
It's like (an apple).
You put (dirty clothes) in it.
You use it to (change TV channels).

Making some time to think in

That's a difficult question.
Well, I suppose that ...
I'm not really sure about that, but I guess ...
I haven't thought about that before, but ...
It's not completely clear in the photo, but perhaps ...

Answer key

Exercise 1

1 got   2 takes   3 at   4 have   5 near
6 do   7 when   8 about

Exercise 2

1 Which one of these do you think would be most useful?
2 I agree that this one is the best *or* I agree that this is the best one.
3 Why don't we choose that one?
4 Perhaps that's not the best way.
5 I guess we'll never agree about this.
6 I see what you mean but I prefer the first one *or* I prefer the first one but I see what you mean.

Exercise 3

1 is   2 years old   3 clothes   4 seem
5 behind   6 come   7 because   8 see

Exercise 4

1 prefer   2 about you   3 not very
4 I'd rather   5 Really   6 Actually
7 because   8 opinion   9 on them
10 I think   11 don't suppose   12 about this

Short message

Example question

An English friend of yours called Julie sent you a birthday present.

Write a postcard to send to Julie. In your card, you should

- thank her for the present
- explain why you like it
- describe what you did on your birthday.

Write **35–45 words** on your answer sheet.

Example answer

Hi Julie — use first names

Thank you so much for the great T-shirt you sent me. — this is the first content point

I love the colour and the size is just right! — this is the second content point

use informal punctuation such as exclamation marks

I had a lovely birthday. My mum cooked a huge meal and all my friends came. We missed you!

See you

Pete

this is the third content point

use first names

use a closing expression

use lively language to add interest

Useful language

Thanking
I just wanted to thank you for …
Thank you so much for …
I really appreciate it.

Apologising
I'm really sorry, but …
I'm so sorry that I can't …

Suggesting and recommending
I think the best thing is to …
Why don't you … ?
Let's …

Reminding
You must remember to …
Please don't forget to …

Inviting
I hope you can …
Would you like to … ?

Explaining
I'll be late because I need to …
I like it because …

Exam help: short message

- Read the instructions very carefully.
- Make sure you include all the content points.
- Address your email to the right person.
- Include a suitable closing.
- Check how many words you have used.
- Try to include some interesting vocabulary.
- Check your grammar for mistakes.

Informal letter

Example question

This is part of a letter you receive from an English penfriend.

> I really like going to the cinema. What kinds of film *do* you like? Tell me about them. Why *do* you like them?

- Now write a letter to your penfriend about films.
- Write your **letter** in about 100 words on your answer sheet.

Example answer

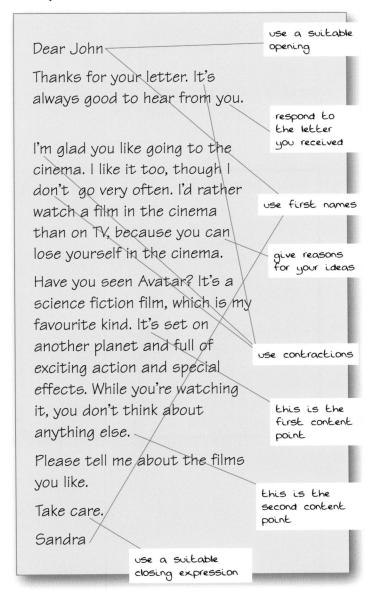

Dear John

Thanks for your letter. It's always good to hear from you.

I'm glad you like going to the cinema. I like it too, though I don't go very often. I'd rather watch a film in the cinema than on TV, because you can lose yourself in the cinema.

Have you seen Avatar? It's a science fiction film, which is my favourite kind. It's set on another planet and full of exciting action and special effects. While you're watching it, you don't think about anything else.

Please tell me about the films you like.

Take care.

Sandra

use a suitable opening

respond to the letter you received

use first names

give reasons for your ideas

use contractions

this is the first content point

this is the second content point

use a suitable closing expression

Useful language

Openings

Dear James,
Hi James,
It's always good to hear from you.
Thanks for your letter.
How are you?
I hope you're well.

To give advice and make suggestions

If I were you …
Why don't we/you … ?
I suggest …
I think you should …
It might help to …
You could try …

To ask for and give information

Could you tell me about …
I need to know …
Let me tell you about …
I thought you'd like to know about …

Giving your opinion

I agree with you that …
In my opinion, …
It seems to me that …
I believe that …
My favourite is …

Closings

Yours
Best wishes.
Write soon.
See you.
Thanks again.
Hope to hear from you soon.
Love

Exam help: informal letter

- Read the instructions very carefully.
- Address your letter to the right person.
- Write your letter in a suitable style.
- Use paragraphs to divide the letter into clear sections.
- Make sure you have included all the content points.
- Try to include interesting vocabulary to make your letter lively.
- Use linking words to join your letter together.
- Count the number of words you have used.
- Try to avoid making spelling mistakes.

Story

Example question

- Your English teacher has asked you to write a story.
- Your story must begin with this sentence:

> I was glad when my phone started to ring.

- Write your **story** in about 100 words on your answer sheet.

Example answer

I was glad when my phone started to ring. I was waiting at the station for Fred. He wasn't on the train that he said in his email, or the one after that. I was bored – two hours is a long time to wait for someone. So I felt happy when I saw that it was Fred's number. But when I answered, he sounded angry! How could he be angry? Soon I became cross too. But you know what happened? He decided to drive to see me in his car. But I never got the email that told me this, so he was sitting outside my house!

use past continuous for background information

include emotions to add interest

use linking words to join your story together

you can ask questions like this to make your story lively

try to have an ending – happy, sad or amusing – to your story

Useful language

Adding interest

At that moment, …
Suddenly, …
Without any warning, …
Then I realised that …

Saying when things happened

It all started when …
A little later …
Meanwhile, …
Some time later, …

Using adjectives and adverbs in descriptions

It was a fantastic concert.
The dinner was absolutely delicious.
I felt completely miserable.
They both felt so scared …
It was a wonderful party.

Bringing a story to an end

It was the best day of my life.
Suddenly, I woke up.
Then I realised it was all over.

Exam help: story

- Read the instructions very carefully.
- If you are given a sentence to use in the story, do not change it.
- Use the names or places that you are given.
- Check your grammar, particularly verb tenses, carefully.
- Make sure you write about the right number of words.
- Use a range of vocabulary and phrases to add interest to your story.
- Divide your story into clear sections with paragraphs.

English Language Club
10th Anniversary

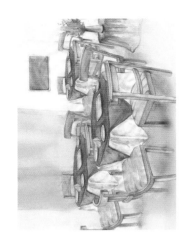

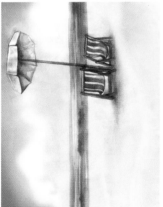

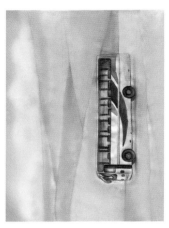

Test 1, Part 3, Photograph 1A

Test 2, Part 3, Photograph 2A

Test 3, Part 3, Photograph 3A

Test 4, Part 3, Photograph 4A

Test 5, Part 3, Photograph 5A

Test 6, Part 3, Photograph 6A

Test 7, Part 3, Photograph 7A

Test 8, Part 3, Photograph 8A

Test 1, Part 3, Photograph 1B

Test 2, Part 3, Photograph 2B

Test 3, Part 3, Photograph 3B

Test 4, Part 3, Photograph 4B

Test 5, Part 3, Photograph 5B

Test 6, Part 3, Photograph 6B

Test 7, Part 3, Photograph 7B

Test 8, Part 3, Photograph 8B

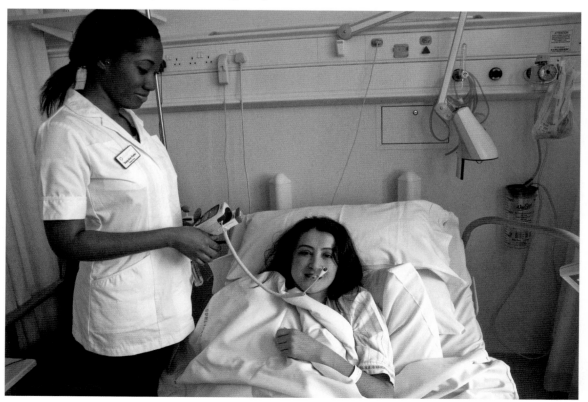

UNIVERSITY *of* CAMBRIDGE
ESOL Examinations

Candidate Name
If not already printed, write name in CAPITALS and complete the Candidate No. grid (in pencil).

Candidate Signature

Examination Title

Centre

Supervisor:
If the candidate is ABSENT or has WITHDRAWN shade here

Centre No.

Candidate No.

Examination Details

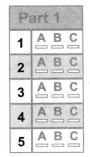

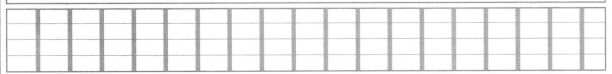
SAMPLE

PET Paper 1 Reading and Writing Candidate Answer Sheet 1

Instructions

Use a PENCIL (B or HB).

Rub out any answer you want to change with an eraser.

For **Reading:**
Mark ONE letter for each question.
For example, if you think **A** is the right answer to the question, mark your answer sheet like this:

0 A B C D

Part 1		Part 2		Part 3		Part 4		Part 5	
1	A B C	6	A B C D E F G H	11	A B	21	A B C D	26	A B C D
2	A B C	7	A B C D E F G H	12	A B	22	A B C D	27	A B C D
3	A B C	8	A B C D E F G H	13	A B	23	A B C D	28	A B C D
4	A B C	9	A B C D E F G H	14	A B	24	A B C D	29	A B C D
5	A B C	10	A B C D E F G H	15	A B	25	A B C D	30	A B C D
				16	A B			31	A B C D
				17	A B			32	A B C D
				18	A B			33	A B C D
				19	A B			34	A B C D
				20	A B			35	A B C D

Continue on the other side of this sheet ➡️

PET RW 1 ∎∎∎ Print Directory Limited 01384 241442   DP491/389

SAMPLE

Part 3: Mark the number of the question you are answering here → Q7 or Q8

Write your answer below.

Do not write below this line

This section for use by SECOND Examiner only

Mark:

0	1.1	1.2	1.3	2.1	2.2	2.3	3.1	3.2	3.3	4.1	4.2	4.3	5.1	5.2	5.3

Examiner Number:

0	1	2	3	4	5	6	7	8	9
0	1	2	3	4	5	6	7	8	9
0	1	2	3	4	5	6	7	8	9

For **Writing (Parts 1 and 2):**

Write your answers clearly in the spaces provided.

SAMPLE

Part 1: Write your answers below.

Do not write here

1	1 1 0
2	1 2 0
3	1 3 0
4	1 4 0
5	1 5 0

Part 2 (Question 6): Write your answer below.

Put your answer to Writing Part 3 on Answer Sheet 2 →

Do not write below (Examiner use only)

0	1	2	3	4	5

©UCLES Photocopiable

UNIVERSITY of CAMBRIDGE
ESOL Examinations

Candidate Name
If not already printed, write name in CAPITALS and complete the Candidate No. grid (in pencil).

Candidate Signature ....

Examination Title

Centre

Supervisor:
If the candidate is ~~ABSENT~~ or has ~~WITHDRAWN~~ shade here

Centre No.

Candidate No.

Examination Details

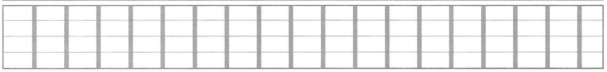

PET Paper 2 Listening Candidate Answer Sheet

You must transfer all your answers from the Listening Question Paper to this answer sheet.

Instructions

Use a PENCIL (B or HB).

Rub out any answer you want to change with an eraser.

For **Parts 1, 2** and **4:**
Mark ONE letter for each question.
For example, if you think **A** is the right answer to the question, mark your answer sheet like this:

| 0 | A̶ B C |

For **Part 3:**
Write your answers clearly in the spaces next to the numbers (14 to 19) like this:

| 0 | example |

Part 1	Part 2	Part 3	Do not write here	Part 4
1 A B C	**8** A B C	**14**	1 14 0	**20** A B
2 A B C	**9** A B C	**15**	1 15 0	**21** A B
3 A B C	**10** A B C	**16**	1 16 0	**22** A B
4 A B C	**11** A B C	**17**	1 17 0	**23** A B
5 A B C	**12** A B C	**18**	1 18 0	**24** A B
6 A B C	**13** A B C	**19**	1 19 0	**25** A B
7 A B C				

PET L   Print Directive Limited 01384 241442

DP493/391

Preliminary English Test: Top 20 Questions

1 **How many marks are needed to pass the exam?**

To pass the exam with a grade C, you need around 60 percent of the total marks.

2 **Do I have to pass each paper in order to pass the exam?**

No. Each paper doesn't have a pass or fail mark. Your overall grade comes from adding your marks on all four papers together.

3 **Are marks taken off for wrong answers?**

No. This means that, if you're not sure, you should always try to guess – you might be right.

4 **Am I allowed to use a dictionary in the exam?**
No.

5 **In the Reading and Writing paper, Reading Parts 1 to 5 have different numbers of questions: does this mean I get different numbers of marks for each part?**

You get one mark for each question that you answer correctly throughout the Reading parts.

6 **In the Reading and Writing paper, how long should I spend on each part?**

This is for you to decide, Remember that the Reading and Writing are worth the same amount of total possible marks.

7 **In Writing Parts 2 and 3 (letter), what happens if I don't write about all the points listed with bullet points (•)?**

You should write about all the things the task requires. The examiners are looking to see if you can provide the right information and good language.

8 **In Writing Part 3, if I write a letter, what do I do about addresses?**

Nothing. Don't spend time writing an address. If you include one, the examiners will ignore it.

9 **In Writing Parts 2 and 3, what happens if I write too few or too many words?**

The word count is an important guide. It tells you how much to write to do the task. But don't waste time counting every word – just make sure you use about the right number.

10 **In Writing Part 1, what happens if I write more than three words in the gap?**

You will not get the mark, because you will not be answering the question properly.

11 **Generally, in the exam, if I'm not sure about an answer, can I give two possible answers?**

No. If there are two answers, and one of them is wrong, you will not get a mark. So you must decide on one answer to give.

12 **In Writing Part 1, do contractions count as one word or two?**

Two. For example, *mustn't = must + not = two* words.

13 **What happens if I make a spelling mistake in the Writing Parts?**

All spelling must be correct in Writing Part 1. In Parts 2 and 3, spelling is one of several things that the examiner considers when deciding what mark to give you.

14 **What happens if I make a spelling mistake in Listening Part 3?**

It depends. If the examiner can still easily understand what word you meant to write, you will get the mark.

15 **How many times will I hear each recording in the Listening paper?**
Twice.

16 **In Listening Part 3, should I use the words I hear in the recording or is it better to use different words?**

You must write only words (or numbers) that you actually hear in the recording. Also, you must not change these words.

17 **In Listening Part 3, what happens if my answer is too long to fit in the space on the answer sheet?**

Most answers are one or two words or a number. These answers will easily fit in the spaces on the answer sheet. If your answer is longer than this, it is probably either wrong, or you are including too much.

18 **In the Speaking paper, can I take the test alone? Or can I choose my partner?**

You must take the Speaking test with a partner. This is because your ability to discuss things with another student is an important part of what is tested.

19 **For the Speaking paper, is it a good idea to prepare what I'm going to say in Part 1?**

It is, of course, good to prepare well for the exam. But you cannot know exactly what the examiner will ask beforehand, so you must listen very carefully to the examiner, and make sure you answer the questions relevantly.

20 **In the Speaking paper, what if my partner makes a lot of mistakes, or doesn't talk much or talks too much?**

Don't worry about these things. The examiners will make sure you have a fair chance in every situation.

Teacher's Guide and Answer Key

Guidance Test 1

Reading Part 1

1
1 five
2 What the text says.
3 on your answer sheet – or you can write your answer on the question paper, and then copy your answers at the end of the test (but remember this means you might make mistakes when copying).

2
1 **C** a note
2 Probably in your home.
3 'give you the money'; 'this afternoon'.
4 **B** is wrong because Charlie is going to collect the clothes from the dry cleaner's, not take them there.
5 **C** is wrong because it is Charlie who has a suit at the dry cleaner's, not Vera. Vera has a coat there.

3
1 **A** a sign
2 You would probably see this in the school where you studied. You would see the sign in the library, probably near the reception desk next to the entrance.
3 You might choose the books you want to borrow from the library.
4 **C** 'until we have checked your books'

4
1 **C** a postcard
2 You might receive this postcard from a friend or relative when he or she is on holiday.
3 Countryside here's <u>OK</u>. Mountains higher than we expected. Very limited wildlife, though the other people in the group are <u>fun</u> and we have <u>easy</u> transport.
4 Countryside here's OK. Mountains higher than we expected. <u>Very limited</u> wildlife, though the other people in the group are fun and we have easy transport.
5 negative

5
1 **C** an email
2 They are probably friends (or perhaps members of the same family).
3 **B** 'Could you send it to her as soon as you can?'
4 'the guest list'

6
1 **A** a sign
2 in a college where you study or work
3 You usually get food and drink in the canteen. The text doesn't say you can get an ID card from the canteen. Probably (although we don't know), you have to go to an office called Student Services or College Office, or similar, to get an ID card.
4 You can't go into the canteen without your ID card: therefore, you must bring your ID card with you when you use the canteen.
5 The text says the same thing about staff as about students: they have to have their ID cards if they want to use the canteen.

7
1 **B** a phone text
2 at 2 p.m.
3 people from other teams
4 we are going to train together
5 4 p.m.

Reading Part 2

1
1 five
2 a magazine to buy
3 magazines
4 eight
5 which magazine would be most suitable for each person
6 on the answer sheet – but you should make notes about your ideas first, and only write them on the answer sheet when you are sure about the answers.

2
1 architecture
2 people who are interested in architecture
3 special buildings near where he lives
4 Omar is interested in (1) <u>architecture, and wants to know more about it</u> [= architecture]. He (2) <u>would like to meet people with the same</u> [= architecture] <u>interest</u>, and to (3) <u>visit special buildings locally</u>.

3
1 long-distance running
2 her running technique
3 so she can go running with them
4 Cecile is very keen on sport and keeping fit, and <u>particularly enjoys long-distance running</u>. She would like to <u>improve her technique</u>, and perhaps <u>find other people to run with</u>.

4
1 to the countryside
2 walking and cycling
3 things in the countryside
4 Duncan <u>enjoys spending his free time in the countryside</u>, exploring different areas <u>on foot and by bike</u>. He wants to <u>know more about what he sees when he is exploring</u>.

5
1 watching her favourite football team
2 no
3 the history of football
4 Heidi <u>likes going to watch her favourite football team</u>, although she <u>usually has to work at weekends</u>, organising jazz concerts. She's keen to <u>learn about the history of football</u>.

6
1 IT and business
2 modern art
3 no
4 Piotr is <u>studying IT and business at university</u>, <u>but he's very interested in modern art</u>, although <u>he's usually too busy to visit galleries and museums</u>.

7
1 **B** *History is Beautiful*
   Art and music lovers will really enjoy this magazine. It's full of interesting articles about the history of concert music, classical <u>architecture</u> around the world, the development of the great <u>museums and galleries</u>.

D *Green World*
   The busier our <u>city</u> lives become, the more we want to escape to the fields and hills. *Green World* is the magazine to take with you. There's lots of information about birds, animals, trees and <u>plants</u>, together with maps of great bike rides and walks to follow.

G *How We Live*
   <u>Houses, offices, museums, bridges</u> … somebody <u>designed</u> them, somebody <u>built</u> them – but most people walk straight past them. Learn about <u>the structures we live and work in</u>. *How We Live* also contains a list of local associations, so you can share your enthusiasm with like-minded people nearby.

H *Pictures in Your Living Room*
   This is the magazine for today's art lover. Every month there are large high-quality reproductions of famous pictures from the 20th and 21st centuries. Turn your <u>home</u> into an <u>exhibition hall</u> of these masterworks, <u>building</u> up a great collection.

2 G
3 Yes: Houses, offices, museums, bridges … somebody designed them, somebody built them – but most people walk straight past them. Learn about the structures we live and work in. *How We Live* also contains a list of local associations, so you can share your enthusiasm with like-minded people nearby.
4 G

8
3 Question 7
   C *Footloose*
      Are you someone who loves being outside, looking after your body? *Footloose* is the <u>magazine for the outdoor runner who takes their hobby seriously</u>. Professional advice is given, with <u>tips for achieving the best style on long runs</u>. There are also lists of <u>local clubs you can contact or join</u>.
   Question 8
   D *Green World*
      The busier our city lives become, the more we want to <u>escape to the fields and hills</u>. *Green World* is the magazine to take with you. There's lots of <u>information about birds, animals, trees and plants</u>, together with <u>maps of great bike rides and walks</u> to follow.
   Question 9
   A *World of Sport*
      This is <u>the</u> magazine for sports fans! All <u>team sports are covered</u>, with <u>reports on games, in case you miss any</u>, interviews with players and much more. There are lots of photos and special <u>articles on subjects such as the early beginnings of football</u> and baseball clubs in distant places.
   Question 10
   H *Pictures in Your Living Room*
      This is the <u>magazine for today's art lover</u>. Every month there are large high-quality reproductions of famous <u>pictures from the 20th and 21st centuries</u>. <u>Turn your home into an exhibition hall</u> of these masterworks, building up a great collection.

9
1 because it won't tell Duncan about the nature he wants to learn about.
2 because it won't tell her about the history of football, or help her know about games she misses when she's at work.
3 because it's about business and sport, not art.

Reading Part 3

1
1 ten
2 two old ships that are in the UK
3 the text
4 if each sentence is correct
5 yes

2
1 Five sentences are about the *Mary Rose* and five are about the *Golden Hinde*.
2 a) 17
   b) 11
   c) 20
   d) 13
   e) 15
   f) 12
   g) 19
   h) 14
   i) 16
   j) 18

3
11 c
12 e
13 b
14 j
15 g
16 a
17 i
18 f
19 h
20 d

4
11 A
12 A
13 B
14 A
15 B
16 B
17 A
18 A
19 B
20 A

Reading Part 4

1
1 the text and questions
2 mark the correct answer **A, B, C** or **D**
3 four
4 on your answer sheet

2
1 camping
2 he loved it
3 in the countryside
4 no
5 his children

3
1 why
2 life
3 opinion
4 hope
5 would say

4
1 e
2 c
3 a
4 b
5 d

5
1 a) encourage, persuade
  b) no
  c) yes
  d) no
  e) no
2 my family moved from city to city … I still live and work in a big city
3 a night at a site once in a while lets you all get your clothes clean and stock up with food
4 fresh air and water, sunshine, running and swimming
5 a) **A** there's no mention of maps.
     B we don't know if children enjoy camping more than adults.
     D there's no mention of danger.
  b) But, wherever you go, don't pack lots of things: keep it basic and you'll have a better time.

Reading Part 5

1
1 the text
2 the correct word for each space
3 four
4 on your answer sheet

2
1 factual (some texts for this part are stories)
2 no, the texts in this part are easy to follow
3 no
4 short

3
1 between
2 place
3 like
4 may
5 be
6 more
7 using
8 say
9 suitable
10 designed

4
1 behind
2 part
3 so
4 must / should
5 have
6 much
7 making
8 inform / tell
9 successful
10 invented

Writing Part 1

1
1 five, and an example
2 a place called Machu Picchu
3 complete the second sentence so that it means the same as the first
4 one, two or three
5 on your answer sheet (but see 7)
6 only the missing words
7 on the exam paper

2
1 They never forget it.
2 They always remember it.
3 yes

3
1 that it is probably the most important historical site in South America.
2 *Other historical sites in South America are probably not ....* *as Machu Picchu.*
3 as important

6
0 b / g
1 e
2 c / f
3 h
4 a
5 d

7
1 When I was younger, I ~~use~~ **used** to go camping.
2 I drove all the way there ~~by~~ **on** my own.
3 I succeeded in ~~repair~~ **repairing** my bike this morning.
4 A classmate of ~~me~~ **mine** lent me this book.
5 ~~I'm~~ **I've been** here for an hour.

Writing Part 2

1
1 a postcard
2 your English friend, Julie
3 three
4 between 35 and 45
5 on your answer sheet

2
1 because Julie sent you a birthday present.
2 *Suggested answer:* Thank you very much for the lovely book you sent me.
3 *Suggested answer:* It's very interesting. The present simple tense.
4 *Suggested answer:* I spent the day on the beach. The past simple tense.

3
1 B
2 B
3 A
4 B
5 A
6 A

4
0 b
1 f
2 a
3 d
4 g
5 e
6 c

5
1 d
2 c
3 a
4 e
5 b

Writing Part 3

1
1 one
2 about 100
3 on your answer sheet
4 in the box at the top of your answer sheet

4
1 that you like
2 so much
3 a little strange
4 more than hear
5 always seems to
6 one if you can
7 with more news

5
1 had forgotten
2 across the room
3 had left
4 fell over
5 banging noise
6 and carefully
7 been here for

Listening Part 1

1
1 four
2 twice
3 look through the questions
4 check your answers
5 on the question paper
6 copy your answers onto your answer sheet
7 six minutes

2
1 seven
2 three
3 choose the correct picture and put a tick in the box below it

3
1 they show two boys
2 the colour of their hair and their clothes (T-shirt and jacket)

4
1 because both the boys have dark hair, and one has a T-shirt while one is wearing a jacket
2 because it shows blonde boys
3 because it shows both boys with T-shirts

5
1 eight o'clock, eight p.m./a.m., eight fifteen, quarter past eight, eight thirty, half past eight

2 pictures of a horse, a tiger and an elephant
3 Go right after you step out of the house, walk straight and turn left at the second crossing; Go right after you step out of the house, take a left at the first corner and then a right; Go left after you step out of the house, turn right on the corner and then left.
4 one or two cartons of (fruit) juice, two or five oranges, a newspaper
5 towels, toothbrush, (travel) clock
6 in **A**, a lorry is hanging off a bridge; in **B**, a tree has fallen and is lying across the road; in **C**, water has flooded in the street and a car is stuck in the water.
7 A shows a shower (for washing or taking a shower); B shows a dishwasher for washing plates and glasses and saucepans, etc.; C shows a washing machine for washing clothes.

6
1 till
2 for / farm
3 have / ahead
4 couple
5 never / only
6 fallen / behind
7 plates / like

Listening Part 2

1
1 six
2 an interviewer and a man called Ronald Ferguson
3 about walking a long way in Scotland
4 put a tick in the correct box
5 twice

2
1 b
2 b
3 a
4 a
5 b
6 b

3
1 A the last day C some days
2 A hills B a week before
3 B in the east, in front of him C as he went further east
4 A when he finished the walk C once
5 A he loved it B it was great seeing them
6 B it starts tomorrow C yes

4
1 Mostly
2 every / before
3 helps / along
4 night / put
5 myself / else
6 then / thought

Listening Part 3

1
1 a teacher
2 a school trip
3 write the missing information in the gaps
4 twice

2
1 a subject
2 a noun
3 a noun
4 a noun
5 a type of transport
6 a type of accommodation

3
14 politics
15 transport
16 medicine

17 wildlife
18 train
19 hostel

4
1 studying
2 improve
3 period
4 projects
5 around
6 spend

Listening Part 4

1
1 six
2 two
3 Max
4 Jenni
5 dinner in a restaurant with their class
6 tick the box **A** or **B**
7 twice

2
1 20 and 23
2 22 and24
3 21 and 25
4 22

3
1 soon
2 pizza
3 the Bamboo House
4 Jenni's parents
5 the Mexicali
6 good things
7 20
8 no
9 list

4
20 d
21 b
22 e
23 a
24 f
25 c

5
1 We really must book the restaurant soon.
2 I see what you mean.
3 What about you?
4 Yeah, that could be a problem.
5 That's a good idea.

Speaking Part 1

1
1 c
2 f
3 h
4 d
5 a
6 g
7 j
8 e
9 b
10 i

Speaking Part 2

1 a
2 c
3 b
4 e
5 d
6 e
7 a
8 b
9 c
10 e

Speaking Part 3

1 see
2 sure I
3 may
4 some
5 so
6 seem
7 tell
8 there's
9 later
10 for

Speaking Part 4

1 because that's the time
2 each other
3 for example
4 Sometimes
5 If
6 and maybe
7 really depends on
8 to do that
9 what I want
10 I guess

Test 1

Photocopiable answer sheets are on pages 189–191.

Reading

Part 1

1 C *Wait in this area* = Do not leave here; *while your books are checked* = until we have checked your books.
2 B *Very limited* = disadvantage; *wildlife* = animals.
3 A *the guest list for the party* = who's going to the party; *send it to her* = let Paula know.
4 B *cannot use the canteen without ID cards* = staff must bring their ID cards if they want to use the canteen.
5 C *This week … we'll have to train at 4 instead [of 2]* = We must go training at a later time.

Part 2

6   G   *Houses, offices, museums, bridges … somebody designed them; Learn about the structures we live and work in; a list of local associations, so you can share your enthusiasm with like-minded people nearby.*

7   C   *magazine for the outdoor runner who takes their hobby seriously; Professional advice is given, with tips for achieving the best style; lists of local clubs you can contact or join.*

8   D   *escape to the fields and hills; lots of information about birds, animals, trees and plants; maps of great bike rides and walks to follow.*

9   A   *team sports are covered, with reports on games, in case you miss any; special articles on subjects such as the early beginnings of football.*

10   H   *for today's art lover; large high-quality reproductions of famous pictures from the 20th and 21st centuries. Turn your home into an exhibition hall of these masterworks.*

Part 3

11   A   *he took control of the town of Boulogne. In response, in 1545, a large number of French ships set sail for England.*

12   A   *Henry VIII, although getting old and ill, came down to take charge of the battle himself.*

13   B   *it sank. There are several different ideas about why this happened, and one day we may know for sure.*

14   A   *Henry tried to have the* Mary Rose *brought up from the seabed.*

15   B   *1982, when she was lifted by the Mary Rose Trust … After some years … Now visitors can view … in the Mary Rose Museum.*

16   A   *three-year voyage around the world, with the Golden Hinde being the only ship to return home safely.*

17   A   *Drake captured many Spanish ships during the voyage, and took their gold and money. When Drake came back to England, he became both rich …*

18   A   *She decided that the ship should be kept so that the general public could come and look at it.*

19   B   *The ship you can visit nowadays is a fully working model of the sixteenth-century ship.*

20   A   *you can become an officer on board and find out how to navigate the* Golden Hinde *in the way the original sailors did.*

Part 4

21   B   The writer's recommending camping and he says it's good to go as a family. He doesn't recommend children go alone, or provide detail about his childhood camping or tell you exactly what to take.

22   D   *my family moved from city to city … I still live and work in a big city.*

23   A   *a night at a site once in a while lets you all get your clothes clean and stock up with food.*

24   A   *I like to think that they understood the value of fresh air and water, sunshine, running and swimming.*

25   C   *don't pack lots of things: keep it basic and you'll have a better time.*

Part 5

26   D   (structural)
27   D   (lexical)
28   A   (structural)
29   B   (lexical)
30   D   (lexical)
31   C   (structural)
32   C   (lexical)
33   A   (lexical)
34   B   (lexical)
35   A   (lexical)

Writing

Part 1

1   as / so important
2   was hidden
3   are
4   (very / rather / quite) slowly
5   unless it

Listening

Part 1

1   C   Boy: *the film isn't till half past, is it?*
      Girl: *No…*

2   C   *I think the elephant is the one to go for, because it's another wild animal.*

3   A   *I turn right when I come out of my house, and then go on till I have to go left, and then school's just ahead along the road.*

4   C   *orange juice for the party … a couple of cartons? … Great. And could you pick up a paper for me too?*

5   B   *I never put my toothbrush in.*

6   B   *A tree has fallen across the street.*

7   B   *I turned it on, so that I could wash the plates, but now water's coming out of it.*

Part 2

8   B   *Some days … Mostly it was around 13 miles. And the last day …*

9   C   *I took fitness classes nearly every day, and did a long walk a week before.*

10   A   *It means you're walking towards the east. The wind generally comes from behind you, so it helps you – sometimes it was so strong it blew me along!*

11   B   *I generally put it up close to the path, wherever I was walking.*

12   C   *the best thing was having some time to myself, with no one else around.*

13   A   *I had the idea of writing a book about walking in Scotland, and I thought about that most of the time.*

Part 3

14   politics
15   transport
16   medicine
17   wildlife
18   train
19   hostel

Part 4

20   B   *Pizza … I eat it at least twice a week. I think it'd be good to have something different.*

21   A   *It's closing next week for a month … So it won't be open for our dinner.*

22   B   Jenni: *I never went there. What about you?*
      Max: *Nope.*

23   A   *I remember going to some place with a singer and guitarist, and it was great. I think we need music.*

24   A   Jenni: *Why don't we fix the amount and ask a restaurant to provide a meal for that price? Then everyone will know exactly how much it's going to cost them.*
      Max: *That's a good idea.*

25   B   Jenni: *don't forget we offered to find out about restaurants and make the decision ourselves – we've got to do the whole job!*

Test 2

Photocopiable answer sheets are on pages 189–191.

Reading

Part 1

1. C *Tell me if you need some more information about it.* = to give him some details.
2. B £30 TO RESERVE ANY PHOTOGRAPH = We will keep a photograph for you, if you pay £30.
3. A *about your new job. Brilliant! I'm sure you're pleased!* = Offering Elsa her congratulations.
4. C *After next Thursday* = from Thursday; *the Study Centre will be closed during evenings and weekends* = change its opening hours.
5. C *it doesn't matter: this one's actually nearer the beach – where I'm spending all my time!* = She thinks it has an advantage.

Part 2

6. D *Follow the joys and heartaches of a junior dance school's attempts to reach the national final championships in different styles; Every afternoon.*
7. F *The white frozen landscape of the South Pole is said to be the last place man hasn't damaged beyond repair. Watch the fascinating filming of native animals and birds.*
8. E *An enjoyable biography of one of the fastest cyclists of all time. Mixing old sections of film with current interviews – and even the chance to phone in with your own questions about technique.*
9. G *celebration of plays and operas, each one performed to the highest standards and broadcast to your living room.*
10. B *strange experiences as he rides around the world on his old red bike, following routes nobody's tried before. Tonight he meets a bear.*

Part 3

11. A *they are qualified fitness trainers, so they will make sure you cycle in the right way.*
12. B *special local foods for your lunch, so you can buy what you prefer.*
13. A *And don't worry about trying to carry all your luggage on your bike, as this will be taken from hotel to hotel in our cars*
14. A *The distance we cover each day will depend on the kind of countryside we're travelling through.*
15. B *a rest by the side of a lake.*
16. B *good-quality 3-star hotels. Experience has taught us that this is the standard most people prefer.*
17. A *single accommodation is available for a small extra payment.*
18. A *in the evenings, you can help yourself from a buffet or go for the set menu.*
19. A *we don't run holidays with fewer than six guests or more than fifteen.*
20. B *these holidays aren't suitable for children under the age of fourteen.*

Part 4

21. D The writer talks about how much design is on TV, about how design has always been part of our lives – from transport to eating. He doesn't try to persuade readers to apply to become designers themselves; he doesn't describe step by step how design has developed through history; he doesn't explain any reasons why certain people don't like design.
22. A *a lot of IT designers seem to think they are kings or emperors, that their work is the most interesting work there is.*
23. B *they float, they move in the right direction,* and *they have pretty patterns, nice colours. We want things to look good and work well.*

24. C *In the West, people have knives and forks; in the East, they have chopsticks – unlike each other in appearance.*
25. D The writer mentions thinking about the history of design, about comparing ancient and modern designs, about comparing designs from different cultures, about design as looks and design as a way of working.

Part 5

26. B
27. A
28. C
29. A
30. D
31. D
32. A
33. B
34. C
35. D

Writing

Part 1

1. the tallest
2. of his / of Ian / of Ian's
3. has
4. used
5. gave him / gave Ian

Listening

Part 1

1. C *You can stand on the little bridge and watch the water flowing. My brother's always climbing the big tree that's by the side of the house.*
2. C *basketball was introduced recently.*
3. A *put it in my jacket pocket.*
4. C Boy: *Yes, she went back home the day before yesterday.* Girl: *The seventeenth?*
5. B Man: *So, who's this, in the centre?* Woman: *That's my parents, when they were middle-aged, of course, with us three girls lined up on the left.* Man: *So who's the old man next to your parents?* Woman: *My grandfather, and then that's my uncle on the right.*
6. A *I just bring a nice magazine*
7. B *because my dad's friends with one of the directors I can get a discount, so that makes it twelve pounds.*

Part 2

8. C *May till September, when I went – is quite pleasant, with warm days, although you do have to remember it gets jolly cold at night.*
9. A *I took a flight in a micro plane on my first day.*
10. B *Suddenly and unexpectedly, there was a lizard.*
11. A *It was lovely when we came across a baby elephant drinking from a watering hole. I think I could have touched him!*
12. C *I think retired people really should get out there and make the most of it.*
13. C *I'll always remember that feeling of so much space, in all directions.*

Part 3

14. 13 July / July 13 / July 13th / 13/07 / 07/13
15. library
16. 10-15 / 10.15 / 10:15 / quarter past ten
17. food
18. the football match
19. high jump

Part 4

20 A   *you haven't got more hobbies – your friends seem to have lots of different things they like doing.*

21 A   *they're just things you do inside, you know, collecting stamps, I mean so boring, or like computer games. I'm just not interested in that kind of thing.*

22 B   *I used to be, but now I'm completely out of practice. I'd lose to anyone.*

23 A   *I went everywhere by bike, and that was good fun.*

24 B   *I don't think that's a good solution. You need to make your own arrangements, find places where you can go safely, that are outdoors.*

25 A   Mother: *Why don't you use all that pocket money we give you, and get yourself a better bike?*
Son: *That's not a bad idea, Mum.*

Test 3

Photocopiable answer sheets are on pages 189–191.

Reading

Part 1

1 B   *Please put all practice equipment back* = You shouldn't take any equipment outside this room; *before you leave* = when you go.

2 B   *with Chris, who's at a job interview at the moment* = Jenny is writing this text while Chris attends an interview.

3 C   *offers welcome (not less than €100)* = Abdul would accept €100 for his bike.

4 A   *Customer parking permitted at any other time* = Customers may park here when vehicles are not unloading.

5 C   *student identity cards will be available for collection from 25 September* = The first day students can pick up identity cards is 25 September.

Part 2

6 G   *for people who have a basic understanding of business, but who want to explore the possibilities of TV, newspapers, the internet and so on as their career; This is a part-time course, with classes three afternoons a week.*

7 B   *High street or street market, clothes, furniture or jewellery: whatever you sell, you can learn to sell more of it; this evening course in IT systems.*

8 A   *you'll learn how to manage others, and bring out the best in any group; relevant to … sports; It's a full-time and demanding course.*

9 H   *Do you wish to be your own boss? Need to know how? Many ambitious and skilled people find they have some experience and perhaps a strong academic background, but feel they need specific knowledge about marketing and finance to ensure their success when selling to the public.*

10 F   *Are you creative? Are you ambitious? This course will help you get ahead in the competitive world of creative business; our course of morning classes.*

Part 3

11 B   *Associate membership gives you half-price tickets to events.*

12 B   *Most of our members have joined as the result of recommendations from current members.*

13 A   *Simply email your question to <u>advice@cameraclub.com</u> or leave a recorded message on 0800 565656. We guarantee to send you a reply by email within five days.*

14 B   *Please note that we cannot provide information about repairs to particular cameras, and that you should contact the manufacturer about these.*

15 A   *Entries can only be accepted from members.*

16 A   *The topic – for example, wildlife, transport, people – is announced each year here on the website.*

17 B   *All full members can send in up to six photos each month.*

18 A   *More photos are added every month.*

19 A   *Our blog space is everybody's chance to have their say. Read articles by other members and learn about new techniques for taking that magical picture or hear opinions on new cameras. You can post your own comments too.*

20 A   *We even offer the choice of 12-hour Super Express service for a small extra charge.*

Part 4

21 C   *John Knight tells us about what he does in his job, what it involves. He's not trying to persuade people to use him as their architect; he doesn't talk about either good or bad architecture; he doesn't talk about other jobs apart from architecture.*

22 D   *My mum and dad suggested I train as an architect, and I just went along with their idea.*

23 B   *Clients – our word for customers … they say they want – and they usually know that very definitely.*

24 B   *the job I'm really hoping to get is the new intercity station.*

25 A   *I invite them to explain the project as they see it developing, and then try to explore ways forward from there.*

Part 5

26 C
27 C
28 C
29 B
30 D
31 A
32 D
33 B
34 C
35 A

Writing

Part 1

1   so
2   first time
3   enough
4   was only
5   is / is very

Listening

Part 1

1 B   *Volleyball was really good fun, and I got much better at getting the ball close over the net.*

2 C   *When I finish in the office, I'll go straight to the gym for about half an hour.*

3 A   *When you come in, you see the living area to the left. You've got the bedroom straight ahead, with the bathroom on the left of that.*

4 B   Girl: *Shall we try for half past?*
Boy: *Yes, it makes more sense.*

5 A   *Both these other ones are the right length I think, and this is the one to go for, because I like the fact that it doesn't have buttons.*

6 C   *the castle with all that lovely cool water round it. So let's get this one with a picture of that.*

7 C   *I've booked us tickets on the train.*

Part 2

8 C   *Once I completed my studies, unemployment was high, and being a courier was the only thing I could find to do.*

9 B *Their office was on this tiny street that didn't even show on my map, and I got really lost.*

10 C *I went to the place I was supposed to take it to, not get it from.*

11 A *very keen – who's the fastest to such and such a place, who's done the most deliveries in one day, that sort of thing.*

12 B *It's not as friendly as people think it will be when they start. You don't necessarily get to know the other couriers very well, because you're coming and going all the time.*

13 B *try it, give yourself say six months to do it.*

Part 3

14 1962
15 visitors
16 farming
17 jam
18 dance
19 £18.50(p)

Part 4

20 B *I really want to go to Scotland, because we had such a great time there last year, but my parents are against it.*

21 A *I've heard you can go skiing in Scotland, so I'd love to go there and try that.*

22 B *My brother's going camping with some college friends, so my parents have suggested I invite a friend along.*

23 A *I'm looking forward to using my new camera; and I enjoy it; Holidays are a good time to try, though.*

24 B *my mother actually, she's always going on at me, saying how I should take the chance to do some reading; It's not as if she follows her own advice either.*

25 A *do you think they'll remember how to relax? They're so hard-working, they'll probably spend the whole time checking their emails or something. I want them to have fun.*

Test 4

Photocopiable answer sheets are on pages 189–191.

Reading

Part 1

1 A *you'll be late for the match. Go on the A15 instead* = Pete needs to change route to arrive earlier.

2 B *We need you to translate* = Help everybody communicate.

3 C *Introduce a friend to the club and receive free sports clothes! Your friend must pay 12-month fee.* = You can get a gift if you persuade a friend to join Goodlife.

4 C *Doug … might be able to get us tickets so let him know if you want to see her play.* = contact if she wants to see the concert.

5 C *at four-hourly intervals* = you must … wait four hours before taking it again.

Part 2

6 B *This music website caters to all tastes; current world music, you should be able to buy what you want here. Many songs are available to listen to for free, and there are some reasonably priced CDs, with an efficient present-ordering service.*

7 A *to music lovers with a taste for the tunes and songs of the dance halls in the middle of the last century. If you're looking for something that's not available elsewhere, or if you'd like to listen to parts of those old favourites for free, try here.*

8 C *a comprehensive guide to all concerts every night, from the large classical shows to the small upstairs blues rooms. What's more, there are plenty of discounts to be had, from half-price entrance to shows to 10 percent off their express CD order line.*

9 E *articles about finding a job in the music business; a playlist facility, so you can put together hours of free listening to download.*

10 G *just right for you if dance is what you like; cheap tickets to see old and new ballet. There's a playlist facility which you can link to your MP3 player and there are articles about ballet's history.*

Part 3

11 B *this site … more environmentally responsible than the paper magazine we used to deliver free to houses, hotels and so on.*

12 B *a new hotel is being built near the centre, and the old Market Hotel is building 20 new rooms.*

13 B *14 July will see Heltonbrook's first Sports Day.*

14 A *Judges will include Greg Davids, our neighbourhood Olympic gold medallist.*

15 A *Please note the closing date is 11 July.*

16 B *over 3,000 works of art by 800 artists. But what's really special about it is the prices: all the art is affordable, with pictures limited to £999.*

17 A *There will be an election – open to all who attend the Show – to decide the single best picture of all.*

18 A *Open Spaces … This special feature of Heltonbrook life runs for a week, from 11–17 July.*

19 A *each year a few more places are added to the list of Open Spaces.*

20 A *See the <u>special programme</u> for <u>details</u> … please note that there may be special conditions for some locations, such as no wheelchair access, for example.*

Part 4

21 B The writer talks about learning on your own, in classes and with the help of technology. The writer doesn't spend the main part of the text recommending one special way of learning languages; the writer doesn't try to persuade people to study harder; the writer isn't requesting information about language learning, but is giving this information.

22 C *taught herself everything she knew.*

23 A *she could communicate in these different cultures. She usually found out more about the people she was talking to than they did about her! … my grandmother has still got it right.*

24 D *feedback facilities on web learning sites helps you to control how you speak, and so improve.*

25 B *there's a lot of extra help these days from IT … I still think going to class means you can interact with other, real people in the same space … It's good to combine these methods.*

Part 5

26 A
27 B
28 D
29 C
30 C
31 B
32 B
33 A
34 D
35 C

Writing

Part 1

1 don't we / do we not
2 hadn't attended / had not attended / had never attended
3 so
4 unless
5 to

Listening

Part 1

1   C   *I'm going to the art gallery to see the sculptures.*
2   A   *The party'll be on the fourth.*
3   A   *he wanted to be standing while she sat.*
4   C   *The championship football match, due to finish at nine, isn't going to finish until nine thirty.*
5   A   *Girl: I think we should get a backpack …*
          Boy: That's agreed then.
6   B   *Man: I think I can get the eleven thirty.*
          Woman: Well, that's the last one.
7   A   *the thick fog that's causing everyone such problems this morning.*

Part 2

8   B   *I went to stay with my grandfather for a few weeks. He had an enormous toy train set, a real kids' dream, and we spent hours playing with it. I've been fascinated ever since.*
9   A   *I'm the Steam Railways Club's chairman.*
10   C   *in 1969, it was the turn of this line, which then sat unused for quite a few years.*
11   B   *In 1990, we were happy to be transporting real passengers for the first time.*
12   C   *Starting this month, you'll also be able to have lunch or dinner on one of our trains. We've nearly finished getting the kitchen ready.*
13   C   *We're glad that our trains and this station are in active use, rather than just preserved in a museum. It's that sense of the past living on through these trains that makes us really proud.*

Part 3

14   money
15   friends
16   personal
17   interview
18   skills
19   countryside

Part 4

20   A   *one of my friends was saying what a great range of clothes you had here.*
21   B   *I actually only joined about a year ago.*
22   B   *My sister said she was trying to choose one for me, for my birthday, but she couldn't decide, so she's given me the money instead, with strict instructions to spend it on a jacket.*
23   B   *leather ones. My own feeling is that they can be rather heavy, rather hot in warm weather.*
24   A   *We are getting a delivery of some new styles; They should be here tomorrow.*
25   A   *I could take something off that for you, say ten percent?*

Photocopiable answer sheets are on pages 189–191.

Reading

Part 1

1   C   *Cyclists – leave road and join pavement, but look out for pedestrians!* = be careful (there are people walking on the pavement).
2   A   *Brian's decided to attend the advanced guitar class … and hopes you will too.* = hopes you will attend the advanced guitar class.
3   A   *This window is only for* = collecting tickets you have reserved.
4   B   *Would you like me to* = an offer; *you've got a problem* = Darragh has a problem, not Hannah.
5   B   *Details from ticket office* = Passengers should enquire in the ticket office; *many are cancelled* = not all trains are running.

Part 2

6   F   *our steaks; if you're short of time … we'll make sure you leave when you need to; We're right in the centre of the city; are open from midday until late.*
7   C   *Whether or not it's a special occasion; Situated in a 17th-century farmhouse; in an attractive village within easy reach of the city; fish … dishes; noon until midnight.*
8   A   *to taste what the Middle East has to offer; not far from the stadium; how little a good meal can cost; Open 9 a.m. till 4 p.m. every day.*
9   H   *food from all over Africa; close to the city art gallery; open for lunch seven days a week.*
10   D   *Right in the heart of the city; vegetarian restaurant; a meal to remember; Open every day, except Sunday, 11 a.m. to 11 p.m.*

Part 3

11   A   *This year we are offering a record number of languages, with the addition of Greenlandish, Farsi and Catalan.*
12   B   *last year, Mandarin Chinese overtook French to attract the largest number of students.*
13   B   *You can take a beginners' course in any language.*
14   A   *You can study two or three languages at the same time, though … the demands of the timetable may make certain choices impossible.*
15   A   *We also offer courses in interpreting and translation between certain languages and English.*
16   B   *it's extremely useful to spend a few months in a country where the language is spoken. So if you can, we encourage you to do this.*
17   B   *We will … advise you about ways of finding accommodation. You will then need to make your own arrangements.*
18   B   *Most of them speak the language they teach as their first language.*
19   B   *Whatever your reason, you'll find that our courses are designed with your needs in mind.*
20   A   *Saville can set up meetings for you with businesses that need your skills. Several major organisations come to us first when they're looking for new employees with foreign language skills.*

Part 4

21 A The writer mentions his first visit to the theatre, and explains why he did the lighting for Clevedon Drama Club. He doesn't mention the club's history, and isn't encouraging people to help the club – he only refers to some of the help that's provided, e.g. costumes. He says he will be acting in the next production, but doesn't say what it is or encourage readers to go and see it.

22 C *my father writes plays in his spare time. He keeps sending them to publishers … they always come back with a polite note saying 'No, thank you'.* So his father's ambition is to get his plays published, but he always fails.

23 B *they had a problem … Nobody else in the club could take over, and my father asked me … I agreed.*

24 C *good lighting … can suggest danger, it can make the audience feel cheerful or relaxed. I found that very exciting!*

25 A *I can never say no to a challenge; it took a lot of hard work; I certainly learned … I found that very exciting! I'll be appearing on stage for the first time!*

Part 5

26 A (lexico-structural)
27 D (lexical)
28 B (lexical)
29 C (lexical)
30 A (structural)
31 C (lexical)
32 A (structural)
33 D (lexical)
34 C (structural)
35 B (lexical)

Writing

Part 1

1 carefully
2 driving
3 more helpful than
4 few
5 as / so good as

Listening

Part 1

1 C *it's going to be wet tomorrow.*
2 B Man: *I've decided to learn the violin …*
Woman: *That sounds like a good idea! I think I'll join you.*
3 A Woman: *Don't you usually get home from work at 6?*
Man: *Yes, and I did yesterday.*
4 C *we wanted two bedrooms and there's only one … there's a small office … It would be nice to have a separate dining room, but we'll eat in the kitchen.*
5 C *maybe you'd like to meet for something to eat first?*
6 B *a field where the cows were grouped together and so were the trees.*
7 A Woman 2: *They were in the fitting room.*
Woman 1: *… I put them on the chair.*

Part 2

8 B *Street Dancing, which was due to be shown on Saturday afternoon. Unfortunately, it couldn't be.*
9 C *It was worth watching, though, in particular because it showed plants growing on rubbish tips, empty garages and other strange places, and not in gardens or the countryside, as in most programmes about plants.*
10 A *the current series started in October, and you'll be sorry to hear that it's now finished.*
11 C *Normally the questions are sent in by the public, but in Sunday's programme some were asked by members of the studio audience.*
12 A *Now I've often been disappointed with Police Officer Briggs … I almost decided never to watch Briggs again … Sunday evening's programme was one of the most exciting I've ever seen.*
13 B *she didn't reach the studio until after the programme ended.*

Part 3

14 lake
15 singing group
16 12.30
17 hills
18 camera
19 lunch

Part 4

20 A *we lived in New Zealand for the last two years, but my father has just got a job here, and we came back.*
21 A *I don't think any of the other schools in the city are as good as this.*
22 B *I'm in Year 8, so I'll have to join the other orchestra.*
23 B *I prefer maths and the sciences.*
24 A *we seem to have far more sports lessons each week than we had at my old school. I wish we had just one lesson a week!*
25 A *I've got Spanish next … our teacher's going to play some Spanish music on his guitar this afternoon, so that should be fun!*

Test 6

Photocopiable answer sheets are on pages 189–191.

Reading

Part 1

1 A *final payment* = paying what you owe.
2 C *Three of the books you reserved have arrived and will be held for seven days* = Kelly can collect those three books within the next seven days. *The others are expected next month* = she has reserved other books which haven't yet arrived in the library.
3 B *Once opened* = after opening the bottle; *the medicine in this bottle should be consumed* = you should drink the medicine; *within six months* = no more than six months after opening the bottle.
4 C *look after* = take care of. *Sorry you won't be able to go swimming* = instead of going swimming.
5 A *Children's Science Exhibition* = it is for children; *Machines have buttons* = The machines are designed; *which should be pressed to make them start* = so that they can be operated.

Part 2

6 B *Join a group of mostly young people; a lively holiday; Spend the day swimming, diving or sailing; There are plenty of places to eat and dance; any number of weeks, from one to four.*

7 E *where to camp and where to buy food; We can also supply tents and the essential equipment for mountain climbing; We recommend at least three weeks.*

8 H *Learn about Mexico from its inhabitants!; You stay as the guest of a Mexican family; up to a week; choose between a city and the countryside.*

9 A *a walk of around 15 kilometres a day, through some of the most beautiful countryside in Italy; a different hotel; your luggage has already arrived; Choose between tours lasting two and four weeks.*

10 F *21 days; cruise ship; The ship offers swimming pool, sports facilities, entertainment and five restaurants; you can go ashore when it calls at ports.*

Part 3

11 B *when the Romans ruled England, two thousand years ago, they constructed many roads. One of them, Ermine Street, runs from London to York, in the north of England. People began to build homes where it crossed the Great Ouse.*

12 B *Huntingdon's first castle dates from 1068, and while many castles of the Middle Ages were built of stone, this one was wooden.*

13 A *the English king ordered that William's castle should be burnt down.*

14 B *Nothing now remains of that castle.*

15 A *One of Huntingdon's inhabitants in the 12th century wrote that the town was … surrounded by forests.*

16 A *King John confirmed Huntingdon's right to hold a weekly market. This was a common way that the kings of England in the Middle Ages raised money, as towns had to pay for the right.*

17 A *visiting traders could stay overnight.*

18 A *you'll be able to … get advice about the fashions of the period.*

19 B *There is no charge for admission to the festival.*

20 A *The Council is aiming to repeat the success of the last festival it organised, in 2005, which attracted over 20,000 visitors.*

Part 4

21 D *Lamarck decided to join the army; he became interested in the natural world; He studied botany, and soon became an expert on the subject; Lamarck became a professor of zoology, the study of animals.* The writer doesn't mention how Lamarck balanced his career and private life, and doesn't make his objectives clear. Although Lamarck changed his job at least twice, there is no suggestion that he lost his job.

22 C *Several of Lamarck's older brothers joined the army, and Lamarck decided to follow them.*

23 A *he collected and took home plants that were not available in France.*

24 B *He developed the idea that different types of animals change over time … Charles Darwin also believed that living things change to fit their environment better. However, Darwin thought Lamarck was wrong about how these changes were caused and he developed his own explanations.*

25 D *He … published a major study of the plants that grew in France; He developed the idea that different types of animals change over time; Darwin thought Lamarck was wrong about how these changes were caused and he developed his own explanations.*

Part 5

26 D
27 C
28 D
29 A
30 B
31 C
32 C
33 D
34 A
35 B

Writing

Part 1

1 on going
2 would / 'd / could go
3 how much
4 as difficult / hard / tough as
5 costs

Listening

Part 1

1 B *I've also applied for a job in a park, and I'd really like that.*
2 C *The jacket's too small – I'll have to go back and change it.*
3 B *the club secretary, Tina Morris, will talk about her recent holiday in Indonesia and show slides that she took there.*
4 A *my son took me to hear a rock band instead.*
5 A *Jill's subject this week is wild animals.*
6 A Man: *maybe some fruit.* Woman: *That's a good idea. I'll do that.*
7 C *I've just got into the school football team, and I have to spend every spare moment practising.*

Part 2

8 A *my friend suggested to the owner that he should call me. He did.*
9 C *I enjoyed it all, except for two or three customers who didn't think they needed to be polite to the waiters.*
10 A *It was hard to find the right place – I wanted it to be in the city centre, not too big, and not too expensive. It was ages before something I liked became available.*
11 B *The waiters … one of them told me he'd never worked anywhere with such a warm, friendly atmosphere – I was really happy about that!*
12 C *customers … But if you don't make them feel they're the centre of attention, and you're happy to see them, they won't enjoy themselves. And then they won't come back, which is bad for business.*
13 A *I don't want to change anything about my work.*

Part 3

14 150
15 having fun / Having Fun
16 history / History
17 movement / Movement
18 14(th) June / June (the) 14(th) / 14/6 / 6/14
19 City Hall / city hall

Part 4

20 A   *she'll be home by the time we get there.*
21 B   *I wish the trip had lasted twice as long.*
22 A   *when I was at school, I went on a cruise on it!*
23 B   *my best friend, Jenny, wanted to go, then the day before we left, she broke her leg, and had to stay at home.*
24 A   *the food was pretty amazing. All except the mushroom soup.*
25 A   *I've bought her one just like the one she lost! Won't she be amazed!*

Test 7

Photocopiable answer sheets are on pages 189–191.

Reading

Part 1

1 A   *Do you have contact details so we can find out* = Claire is asking Jake how to get information.
2 B   When the button lights up, you can press it. This will open the train doors.
3 A   *you're still there* = Will is in Rome; *we can travel to Naples together* = i.e. from Rome to Naples.
4 C   The notice only says that permission is necessary for moving the equipment out of Lab 1.
5 B   *could you take this DVD to Jackie on your way to college?*

Part 2

6 F   *Karin Halvorsen creates strange and exciting pictures in the reader's mind; Halvorsen's skill at writing; one of the best-known … novelists for teenagers.*
7 C   *You won't be able to put the book down until you've reached the last page!; a major bank robbery; fights, murders; amazing surprises.*
8 A   *until we become adults; in earlier centuries; children; the lives of typical children around the world in the last two centuries.*
9 H   *Hussein Al-Djabri lived in Morocco … his father started working in Canada, and the whole family soon followed him; now lives in Germany; novel; a life that is very similar to Al-Djabri's.*
10 E   *in the last five centuries; how science has developed in the same period; People who know little or nothing about the subject will learn a lot from this book.*

Part 3

11 B   *this year we are offering more cruises than ever before.*
12 A   *Southampton, where you will join your ship.*
13 B   *you will call at a number of exciting destinations, depending on the particular cruise.*
14 B   *For an extra charge, you will have time for a three-hour ride on the train.*
15 B   *our visit will be too brief to attend a performance.*
16 A   *Much of Sweden's capital is on islands, and a third of the city consists of water.*
17 A   *the Little Mermaid … This is only a short distance from where you leave the ship.*
18 A   *Like Copenhagen, Helsinki, the Finnish capital, is small enough to explore the historical centre on foot.*
19 A   *you will have two full days in port here.*
20 B   *If you'd like a guided tour, there are plenty available – on foot, by car or by boat along the city's rivers and canals – although unfortunately we no longer organise tours ourselves.*

Part 4

21 A   The writer describes how she started working in hotels, why she decided to continue and the hotel where she works now. She doesn't suggest that readers should become hotel managers, describe the difficulties of working in a hotel or compare hotels of two different periods.
22 D   *making guests feel welcome isn't a question of size but of attitude … It all depends on the employees.*
23 C   *I had to find a job with accommodation.*
24 B   *Before I started at this hotel, almost all its employees left within a year; My main achievement so far is that now only a third do.*
25 B   *making guests feel welcome isn't a question of size but of attitude … It all depends on the employees; 20-room, independent hotel … our restaurant menu attracts both guests and local people.*

Part 5

26 B
27 D
28 A
29 D
30 A
31 C
32 B
33 D
34 B
35 C

Writing

Part 1

1   my dreams
2   for / on
3   I save (up)
4   go
5   such

Listening

Part 1

1 C   *I always walk home.*
2 B   *I was with Marcia … her dad came with us. Oh, and her younger brother, Terry.*
3 A   *if you'd like to see a dentist it's still possible to make an appointment.*
4 B   Woman: *Shall we buy this painting of the woman? …* Man: *OK. We'll buy the one you like.*
5 B   *I've put it where I can reach my books without having to get up.*
6 C   *it's going to be the shopping centre.*
7 A   *A bus travelling south has broken down on the M6.*

Part 2

8 B   *Anyone can take part in the fishing competition, the plastic duck race and several other events.*
9 C   *others built in the style of boats of hundreds of years ago.*
10 C   *make sure you have your breakfast very early! But don't worry – even the slowest runners will finish in plenty of time for lunch.*
11 A   *The light show will begin at sunset, at the harbour, so that's the place to go.*
12 B   *there will also be lots of singers, dancers and circus performers from around the world.*
13 B   *The only way they've managed to get the festival ready was by starting work on it immediately after last year's festival – two months earlier than usual.*

Part 3

14 17
15 (the) table tennis
16 singing
17 hill walking
18 April
19 train

Part 4

20 B *I've only been able to swim for a few months*
21 A *my cousins and I went to the beach every day. One of them could swim really well, and he taught me how to.*
22 A *you have to be very careful in the sea, and make sure it's safe, but I think it's much better with the waves and the beach. I think swimming pools are rather boring.*
23 A Collette: *One day I want to swim across the Channel!*
Robbie: *What, all the way from England to France?*
24 A *I go every Friday after school – more in the holidays.*
25 B Robbie: *Do you want to have a race?*
Collette: *I don't think so – you'll beat me easily!*

Test 8

Photocopiable answer sheets are on pages 189–191.

Reading

Part 1

1 A *let me know* = contact; *the earliest you can manage* = what train they should catch.
2 B *No items of value are left* = valuable items are removed; *outside opening hours* = when it is closed.
3 B *Could you email your mushroom curry recipe, please? I'd like to make it.*
4 A *check in* = let the doctor know that you have arrived.
5 C *your place* = Roland's home; *I'll get there* = she'll go to Roland's home.

Part 2

6 B *World Literature; books you can read in your own time; in the original language or in translation; you decide how much time you spend reading each week.*
7 H *part of a team; do some exercise to keep fit; swimming team; every Saturday morning.*
8 E *Beginner; art at the college; You'll learn to … use oils. Instead of regular classes, one of our tutors will be available every day and evening, so you can come in when it's convenient for you.*
9 F *the whole of every Thursday; fashion and beauty; It prepares you for a range of careers, including hairdressing, fashion design and the theatre.*
10 A *how to repair your own car engine; qualify as a car mechanic; You'll learn how engines are made, and have a lot of practice at repairing them; 9 a.m. until 4 p.m. every Tuesday.*

Part 3

11 A *Cork is the second-largest city in the Republic of Ireland, after the capital, Dublin.*
12 B *Many of these lines have since closed, however.*
13 A *the river Lee … divides into two main channels, creating the island on which the city centre is situated.*
14 B *Ships sail down the river the few miles that separate Cork from the open sea.*
15 A *There are a number of tours each day, every one exploring a different period in the city's history.*
16 B *The tours … take place on Mondays to Fridays, from the beginning of April until the end of September.*
17 A *Just buy a day ticket and you'll be free to get off one bus and get on another as many times as you like during the day.*
18 B *this magnificent building was built to look like a castle.*
19 A *In the 1920s a radio station opened in part of the former prison … the studio that was first used here in 1927.*
20 A *in its early days, English businesses bought food here to resell in shops in England.*

Part 4

21 B *If you're thinking of organising a Harmony Day event, there is a government department which can advise you. In addition, examples are given of different sorts of events.* The writer doesn't ask for suggestions for improvements, introduce a programme for a particular Harmony Day or write about the last Harmony Day.
22 C *The celebrations have even reached across the ocean, with a video link between a school class in Australia and one in Italy.*
23 B *five people chatting about why they had moved, and comparing life in Australia and in the countries where they were born.*
24 D *many of the people there were happy … to have a cultural background from another country.*
25 B *Harmony Day is an annual celebration of this wide range of cultures; thousands of schools, clubs and other organisations have arranged events, and the number is growing; ways of bringing together people from different cultures.*

Part 5

26 A
27 D
28 A
29 A
30 B
31 C
32 B
33 D
34 C
35 C

Writing

Part 1

1 at least
2 than
3 too
4 film attracts
5 less

Listening

Part 1

1 C *their performance on the 21st.*
2 A Woman: *I wanted to visit a city, maybe New York.*
      Man: *So where did you go?*
      Woman: *Where I wanted to go!*
3 A *turn right, then take the first left. We live in the second road on the right, and the door's on the corner.*
4 A *But here's the key I lost last week.*
5 C *For a mobile phone there's 20% off the usual price.*
6 B *It's in the street.*
7 A *I'd really like to go out … We could go somewhere cheap for a burger or something.*

Part 2

8 C *I expect most of you have wanted to be actors since you were children – I certainly have. My parents first took me to the theatre when I was six, and I loved it – the excitement, the magic.*
9 B *while I was here, at drama college, I got a small part in a TV comedy programme: … it was my first job as a professional actor!*
10 A *The sort of roles I'm most interested in playing are those that seem to be totally unlike me.*
11 A *what I strongly recommend that you do – is to talk to strangers, find out what sort of person they are. … I think watching ordinary people is even better.*
12 C *It isn't by anyone you've heard of.* [The friend she mentions directs plays and has read this one, not written it.]
13 C *I'll help you to sell tickets by telling all my friends and other actors about it.*

Part 3

14 side gate
15 8.15
16 toy
17 computer
18 beach
19 North Street

Part 4

20 B *ever since I was five years old, so not quite my whole life.*
21 B *When I was young, I knew most people who lived here, and everyone was friendly … Now there are thousands of people I don't know, and nobody even says hello.*
22 A *the new school's too far away from where most children live. They should have built it closer to the new houses by the river.*
23 A *It's a fantastic building, though. I think it's quite beautiful.*
24 A *we certainly need somewhere like that.*
25 A *I've offered to be on the committee when the leisure centre opens.*